Going Public

Chicago Guides
to *Writing,* Editing,
and Publishing

Going Public

A Guide for Social Scientists

Arlene Stein and Jessie Daniels

Illustrations by Corey Fields

The University of Chicago Press

Chicago and London

The University of Chicago Press, Chicago 60637
The University of Chicago Press, Ltd., London
© 2017 by The University of Chicago
Published 2017.
Printed in the United States of America

26 25 24 23 22 21 20 19 18 17   1 2 3 4 5

ISBN-13: 978-0-226-36464-3 (cloth)
ISBN-13: 978-0-226-36478-0 (paper)
ISBN-13: 978-0-226-36481-0 (e-book)
DOI: 10.7208/chicago/9780226364810.001.0001

Library of Congress Cataloging-in-Publication Data

Names: Stein, Arlene, author. | Daniels, Jessie, 1961– author. | Fields, Corey,
    illustrator.
Title: Going public : a guide for social scientists / Arlene Stein and Jessie Daniels ;
    illustrations by Corey Fields.
Other titles: Chicago guides to writing, editing, and publishing.
Description: Chicago : The University of Chicago Press, 2017. | Series: Chicago
    guides to writing, editing, and publishing | Includes bibliographical references
    and index.
Identifiers: LCCN 2016022230 | ISBN 9780226364643 (cloth : alk. paper) |
    ISBN 9780226364780 (pbk. : alk. paper) | ISBN 9780226364810 (e-book)
Subjects: LCSH: Communication in the social sciences. | Social sciences—
    Authorship. | Sociology—Authorship. | Academic writing.
Classification: LCC H61.8 .S84 2017 | DDC 808.06/63—dc23 LC record available at
    https://lccn.loc.gov/2016022230

♾ This paper meets the requirements of ANSI/NISO Z39.48-1992 (Permanence
of Paper).

Contents

Introduction

So You Want to Go Public?

A few years ago, a *New York Times* columnist railed against professors for glorifying "arcane unintelligibility while disdaining impact and audience." There are "fewer public intellectuals on American university campuses today than a generation ago," Nicholas Kristof declared, implicating academics' turgid prose, weak social media presence, quantitative emphasis, hidden journals, and focus upon technique and abstraction rather than relevance and clear thinking. "Some of the smartest thinkers," he wrote, "just don't matter in today's great debates."[1] And they are themselves largely to blame for this.

Members of the professoriate were furious, and charged that the accusations were unfounded. We are in fact deeply engaged with the world around us, teaching thousands of undergraduates every year, and are actively involved in the communities where we live—Kristof just can't see it—they asserted. But others admitted that the *Times* columnist's complaints were at least partially accurate. Many scholars would like to be more publicly engaged, but they don't really know how to go about doing so. Or they feel their professional commitments compel them to communicate mainly with colleagues, in ways that prevent others from joining the conversation.

A junior scholar laments, "I've been publishing on my research for over ten years but it's been a long and hard struggle to take pride in what I do. I guess part of the shame about my work is that it's so incredibly academic. Though it's my job to write in this way (and I don't always have a choice in the matter), I know that much of my writing can be very inaccessible to the people I care about most, my family, my friends and most of all, the people who are the topic of my research: migrant workers."

She worries that by writing more accessibly she'll lose status in her chosen profession, especially since she's a woman of color who already faces challenges operating in majority-white institutions. "I'm trying to move past this and embrace my role as a scholar and writer with my second book," says the sociologist. "But my fear now is that academic colleagues will think it's unsophisticated and too elementary. (Sigh, yes I have issues!)"[2] She's not alone.

As scholars, we steep ourselves in the theories and methodologies of social research in order to master the tools of our discipline. We believe that such tools offer us a way to systematically understand the world. In the process, we learn the conventions of our field and expectations of what makes for good scholarly work. Later, if we're lucky enough to land a job at a college or university, we are tasked with the challenging work of teaching young minds. Many, if not most of us, also produce social research. In order to publish this work, we must receive the approval of peers who make up the editorial boards of our journals, who review our manuscripts. To do so, we adhere to very high levels of theoretical and methodological rigor, and address audiences comprised mainly of other experts.

During this process, we often begin to shed our distinctive voices. We also learn to distance ourselves from those who do not share our expertise. Being a card-carrying social scientist, we learn, means writing dispassionately and trying very hard to sound smart—

"academic." The process begins early on. In graduate school, we often hear talk that seeks to keep us on track and in line, such as when our professors disparage by saying "this is not sociology," "this is too descriptive," or worse yet, "this is journalistic." But as sociologist Howard Becker, a talented writer himself, admits, "academic journals insist on the most academic prose, for no reason that anyone can explain very well."[3] Ironically, complaints about turgid scholarly writing often come from the very disciplinary gatekeepers who supposedly uphold the standards that constrain us, including officers of professional organizations, journal editors, tenure committees, and dissertation advisors.

Despite the fact that communicating is absolutely central to what we do, collectively we social scientists spend relatively little time reflecting upon how to do it better, and even less time figuring out how to communicate with those outside of our areas of specialization, or with nonacademic publics. A Stanford education scholar worries that the current focus on refereed journal articles has not kept pace with the profound changes in how information is disseminated in modern society. "The university, particularly professional schools that are supposed to be producing knowledge for practitioners, are being left behind," writes Sam Wineburg. "We are becoming less and less relevant to the people who most need our knowledge—teachers and students and principals and decision-makers in the field."[4]

In their search for "relevance," in recent years a number of academics have begun to speak about the importance of public engagement; some have even come to call themselves "public scholars." Self-described "public anthropologists" call upon their colleagues to initiate conversations with "broad audiences about broad concerns" such as rights, health, violence, governance, and justice, instead of setting their sights on narrow problems that concern few people outside the discipline.[5] Noting that nearly all of the income gains during the post-2008 "recovery" in the United States have gone to the top 1 percent, and that median wage for the rest of the population continues to drop, Angelique Haugerud calls upon her fellow anthropologists to participate more vocally in "our era's economic dilem-mas" and reject the "economic simplifications that pervade public discourse."[6] She and others hope to reframe and reinvigorate their discipline by enlarging the scope of academic inquiry and calling upon their colleagues to engage in pressing issues in their communi-ties—and the world. They suggest that it is our responsibility to com-municate our research beyond scholarly circles. Similar initiatives, which are taking place in fields such as sociology, are long overdue.

But such discussions rarely involve nuts-and-bolts advice about *how* exactly to move one's research into public arenas. Even if they are committed to engaging with nonacademic publics, after undergoing years of rigorous graduate training, and being steeped in the profes-sional obligation to publish their research results in peer-reviewed journals or scholarly books, few graduate students, researchers, and professors feel equipped to do so. After spending seven or more years writing a well-researched dissertation, how can one possibly con-dense it into a seven hundred-word newspaper op-ed? After writing six-thousand-word articles for the *American Political Science Review,* how can we begin to engage with something like Twitter, with its re-strictive 140-character limits? And is it worth the trouble?

It doesn't help when peers and professional organizations tell us that public scholarship is something one does "after hours" or—if one is a graduate student or junior professor—after getting tenure. Sadly, graduate departments sometimes send the message that in or-der to be a professional social scientist, one must dedicate oneself exclusively to publishing work that involves rigorous hypothesis testing and theory building, in journals read almost exclusively by other professional social scientists. Few PhD-granting departments believe that they should be teaching aspiring social scientists how to do public scholarship. University-based scholars tend to reinforce that view: some scoff at those who write for a wider audience and consider the moniker "pop sociology" to be an insult. Where are the methodological appendices, they ask? Why don't popularizers ad-equately credit those whose works they draw upon?

Clearly, scholars who are on the tenure track must prioritize the kind of research and publishing their departments require for re-appointment, tenure, and promotion. At the same time, we must acknowledge that the higher education landscape is changing: while institutions continue to produce PhDs, there are fewer tenured or tenure-track positions. More of us are pursuing alternative kinds of academic careers: as long-term adjuncts, full-time but temporary lecturers, independent scholars, or in nonacademic research jobs. Under these conditions, the advice to "wait until tenure" to engage in public scholarship seems less than helpful.

There are other reasons why people shy away from public engagement, even "after tenure." Moving one's scholarship out of academia and into the public sphere may require us to leave our comfort zones, face potential silences, and open ourselves up to unwanted scrutiny or critique. In the age of social media, such critiques circulate quickly and easily, and can become personal ad hominem attacks. Why bother writing that op-ed, if it results in a wider range of people criticizing our ideas? While an academic article may translate into clear professional payoffs and contribute a line to one's curriculum vitae, the rewards that accrue from writing an op-ed or blog post are often less tangible. Why take the time to write a more popular piece when there's that unfinished article sitting on your desk? Why bother learning to do public scholarship when there's so little formal training, it might cause trouble for you, and the professional rewards are unclear?

For us, the answer to these questions is clear: there's a big world out there that needs to hear from us. When those who possess in-depth training and expertise are excluded from public debates about pressing issues such as climate change, work-family balance, and other subjects (fill in the blank!), such discussions are likely to be shaped by corporations, wealthy businessmen with vested interests such as the Koch brothers, or celebrities (recall Jenny McCarthy's and Jim Carrey's forays into the vaccine debate) who can sway public opinion in uninformed ways. There is another good reason for us to become public scholars, too: engaging with broader audiences can make our work better. Bringing others into the conversation before and after publication allows us to test our ideas and make them stronger.

Going public isn't for everyone. There's a time and place to speak exclusively with other specialists in the language of professional social science, to be sure. But undergraduates, journalists, the educated "lay" public, community activists, members of labor movements, religious groups, policy professionals, and others could be very interested in our research—if we learn to communicate it in engaging ways. Can we approach readers on their own terms, and tell intriguing stories about our work? Can we access the expanding array of tools—data visualizations, graphs, photographs, videos, blogs, or even performance—which are available to do so?

This book is a guide for scholars who are interested in communicating with diverse audiences. While *Going Public* is designed specifically for those who wish to broaden their reach to nonacademics, we hope it will aid you in improving your scholarly communication skills, too. We're big fans of Howard Becker's guide *Writing for Social Scientists*, which has helped many a shell-shocked graduate student and young faculty member figure out how to translate their ideas into clear writing. We hope this book will continue the conversation begun by Becker and extend it into the digital era. In addition to helping you take your writing to another level, we will introduce you to some of the new digital tools scholars are using right now. Recognizing that tools come and go, we'll offer principles that will endure beyond specific platforms.

In doing so, we draw upon our many years of experience as academics and public scholars. Arlene has wrestled academic prose into engaging writing as editor of *Contexts*, a magazine of popular sociology, and writes books for general audiences as well as for scholars. Jessie traverses the worlds of academia and high tech, publishes a scholarly blog, and trains social scientists to use the tools of journalism and digital media. We're both social scientists with activist backgrounds. In the process of writing this book, we've talked to friends, colleagues, people who work in the publishing world, and individuals who are actively engaged in the work of public scholarship.

But before we get into the practical task of actually learning how to do public scholarship, let's reflect upon what it means to be a publicly engaged social scientist today. What are some of the challenges we face in doing such work? And what are the institutional structures and professional routines that shape our lives as social researchers and teachers, constraining and offering opportunities for going public?

Academics as Experts

In 2014, when Attorney General Eric Holder called for the repeal of laws that keep millions of people with felony records from voting, he used the work of criminologist Chris Uggen. In a 2010 study, Uggen found that just one in five felons who are eligible to vote actually do so. While there are an estimated 20 million people with felony convictions in the United States, including 1.5 million now in prison, about 5.6 million of these people are forbidden to vote by state laws, a disproportionate number of whom are African American. Law professor Michelle Alexander calls this the "new Jim Crow."

Depending upon where they were convicted, over 13 million people may have either had their voting rights restored or never lost them, even when incarcerated, yet many are under the mistaken impression that they're ineligible to vote.[7] Uggen's research was compelling, important, and timely. "We'd undertaken the project with both science and policy in mind, in hopes of doing good sociology that would also encourage the sort of national conversation now taking place," he says.

On a daily basis social scientists tend to communicate with others like ourselves—mainly through conference papers, journal articles, and books written for other academics. We do our research in tried and tested ways, and then send it out into the academic world, hoping that it will also catch the eyes of journalists, policy makers, and others. Sometimes a university media affairs office, or a publicist at a publishing house, or even a paid publicist pitches in to insure that it does. If we're successful, like Uggen, our work breaks out of academia and enters different public arenas—typically via journalists, who disseminate our research findings to broader audiences.

That's the dominant model of how academics come to participate in conversations about things that matter: climate change, gender inequalities, debates about how to best raise children, and myriad other current issues. It is a model that relies on reporters to translate our work to broader audiences. And it leads, more often than not, to that expert quote; so, for example, in 2013, by one count, at least 124 sociology professors were quoted in news articles, reviews, or op-eds in the *New York Times*.[8] It is an important way academics influence public opinion, to be sure.

Academics tend to subscribe to the model of scholar-as-expert because we see ourselves as holders of privileged insight. After all, we spend a good chunk of our professional lives training for the day when we can call ourselves experts. When we speak in public, we use the mantle of academic authority we've worked long years to display. Many of us wish to make our ideas and findings accessible to a wider audience, and we welcome such attention. It shows us that we are relevant and important. Universities love it, too, when one of their faculty members gets quoted in the press.

This model assumes that academics and the lay public occupy two very different worlds, and relies on journalists to act as a bridge between those worlds, translating scholarly work to lay audiences. It is a model that is the product of the increasing professionalization of scholarly production. At an earlier moment, the boundaries between the academic and nonacademic worlds were somewhat more permeable, which was reflected in the style of writing found in the leading journals of social science: essayistic, dialogical, and marked by the author's presence.

In 1895, in the first issue of the *American Journal of Sociology*, founding editor Albion Small described the goal of the journal as follows: "[This journal will] attempt to translate sociology into the language of ordinary life. . . . It is not . . . essential to the scientific or even the technical character of thought that it be made up of abstractly formulated principles. On the contrary, the aim of science should be to show the meaning of familiar things, not to construct . . . a kingdom for itself" that is "obscured under an impenetrable disguise of artificial expression."[9] During the next few decades, W. E. B. DuBois wrote trailblazing books about black civil rights, the color line, and other topics that crossed disciplinary boundaries and engaged diverse audiences.

And yet, by the middle of the twentieth century social science journals came to look more and more like those in the natural sciences, with their literature reviews, charts, tables, and methodologically driven articles. The movement toward disciplinarity, professionalization, and scientism was rapidly under way, transforming sociology journals into highly specialized publications catering almost exclusively to professional social scientists.

What led to this shift? After World War II, American universities underwent considerable expansion, and members of previously disenfranchised groups were able to gain footholds within it. Striving working-class youth, often from ethnic European immigrant backgrounds, joined what had been an almost exclusively white, Protestant, and upper-class preserve, and to some extent women did, too. The growth of the profession ushered in the rise of more sophisticated methodologies—and also efforts on the part of some of its leading practitioners to differentiate the social sciences from other forms of knowledge, including journalism.

Talcott Parsons, perhaps the most influential sociologist of the mid-twentieth century, in a 1959 address to the American Sociological Association, declared that sociology "is clearly primarily dedicated to the advancement and transmission of empirical knowledge" and only "secondarily to the communication of such knowledge to nonmembers."[10] Organizations such as the American Sociological

Association and the American Political Science Association were established to evaluate social research and build credibility for it. The professionalization of knowledge facilitated the development of sophisticated methodologies for social research, the articulation of rigorous standards, and the development of vehicles for facilitating communication among scholars.

Collectively, we benefit from these routines and structures: they provide space for us to meet with our colleagues and discuss our work in progress and sponsor our publications. The authors of this book make our living as professional sociologists, and we're grateful for the opportunity to do so. But when professionalization encourages us to speak mainly to our academic peers, it leaves the process of translation to journalists—which is not always a good thing.

Caught in the Spotlight

Karen Sternheimer has frequently been consulted by news organizations looking for that telling quote on such topics as why some people are scared of clowns, the cultural importance of "Friday the thirteenth," and why many people don't flush public toilets. "I'm always a bit flattered when asked to comment on a story," the sociologist says, "and have felt a sense of responsibility to cultivate the sociological imagination among a wider audience whenever possible." But she laments that she has often been misquoted or taken out of context.

Once, when asked to comment on how gender is represented on reality television shows, Sternheimer mentioned that such shows are "cast to stoke conflict" and give the impression that women are always in conflict. She said that portrayals of women "as inevitable enemies were anti-feminist, and that they made the possibility of women's collective action seem impossible." In a nationally syndicated article, she was quoted as saying that "women naturally can't get along."[11] Anthropologists similarly lament that when reporters cover conflicts in Africa and the Middle East, or even Eastern Europe at times, they tend to portray them as ancient battles over ethnic divisions, rather than as modern contests over political power and resources. Because of this, when asked to contribute an expert quote, anthropologists can be wary of reporters' tendency to use their words to reinforce the tribal hatred frame.[12] When others frame your research, you risk losing control over your own words.

At times, media outlets hungry for "content" and "click-throughs" (users who click on a specific link) misrepresent research findings to try to appeal to their target audiences of largely middle-class readers and viewers. For example, an article in the *American Sociological Review* showed that children of parents who contribute more money to their college education often receive lower grades than those students who paid more of their own way. It contradicted the widespread belief that the more you give, the better your child does. Sounding the call of alarm, the *New York Times* reported: "Parents beware: The money you contribute to your child's college education may lead to lower grades." The study actually showed a correlation between parental giving and student grades but did not claim that there was a causal relationship between the two.[13]

No wonder academics often have mixed feelings about serving as media experts. Sociologist George Ritzer relates his experience of being vetted by a television producer for a potential appearance on one of the morning talk shows. As he was in the middle of explaining his notions of the "globalization of nothing" and "McDonaldization," Ritzer said, "I could almost feel the producer lose interest." When he finished, the producer said, in effect, "Don't call us, we'll call you," to which the sociologist replied, "Well. I guess my ideas on nothing and its globalization were not 'McDonaldized' enough." The producer laughed and said, "That's right!"[14] Fearing that the media will require us to oversimplify our ideas in order to make them more palatable for consumption by a mass audience, we worry about compromising intellectual rigor.

Social scientists often find that they are "merely hitching on to a juggernaut that uses them up in drive-by quotations on random topics," writes sociologist Pepper Schwartz. If they wish to make a real contribution, scholars must "frame the debate, by creating and interpreting the data more polemically, earlier in the game," she says. Otherwise "we become mere sound bites in someone else's effort to create meaning and policy."[15] The alternative is to allow journalists, or anyone with a website, to frame public debates.

When journalists tell stories about social trends, such as hooking up on college campuses, they tend to tell them through the lives of individuals, offering up scenes and characters. They're neither beholden to professional social scientific codes nor dedicated to producing knowledge that is broadly generalizable. In order to hold on to their jobs, they must write in an appealing, engaging way, holding the attention of their readers. Generally speaking, they see themselves as reporters (as the old adage goes, "Just the facts, ma'am") rather than interpreters, encouraging readers to offer their own interpretations of events.

In contrast, social scientists make arguments that draw on data, in the form of numbers if they're quantitative researchers, or vignettes and thick descriptions if they're more qualitatively oriented. They're more attuned than journalists to questions like, Can we generalize from this one case? Is this particular example broadly representative of the social phenomenon at hand? Rather than appeal to unknown readers, social scientists must please an audience of peers, other professionally trained experts in their field. And adhering to professional research ethics, they must take care to protect their informants' privacy.

Faced with such differences of purpose and audience, some would suggest that we leave storytelling to the journalists, and scholarship to the sociologists, anthropologists, political scientists, and so forth. Let journalists speak to the people while social scientists keep working in the trenches, doing the hard work of data collection and analysis. In other words, one solution to the seemingly unhappy marriage of journalism and social science is to seek a divorce.

Social scientists and journalists inhabit somewhat different worlds, to be sure. We have different conceptions of audience, different ways of collecting "data," and different professional norms. And yet the social sciences and journalism also exist in relation to one another. Journalists regularly consult social scientific experts to make sense of events they report on, and sometimes they enlist them for a telling quote or two. Social scientists know what they know about the world partly from consuming newspapers, television, digital media, and so forth. We live in a media-saturated world, a world where it is difficult, if not impossible, to separate out "reality" from its media representations.

The rise of social media has made the boundaries between academia and journalism even more fluid. Today, more and more scholars have their own social media presence and are less likely to wait around for a journalist to call or e-mail to use their expertise to comment on current events. Through blogs, Twitter, Tumblr, and other social media, scholars are offering their takes on unfolding events as they happen. Journalists are also more likely to identify experts through their online presence. It's become common practice for journalists to mine academics' blogs to find out more about a subject, and to locate a telling quote. For their part, academics can publicly take journalists to task if they publish something that's simply inaccurate.

Becoming Translators

When social scientists are consulted about their research by the media, journalists typically play the role of translators, transforming complex arguments into ones that laypersons can understand. But what if academics cut out the middleman (or woman) and played the role of translator of their research? What if we learned to code switch, communicating our own work both to expert and nonacademic audiences, cutting out the need for someone else to interpret it for nonacademics? What if we did not have to rely on others to translate our work? To do so, we would need to rethink the audience in our heads, transforming it from a finite group of other experts, such as our dissertation committee members, or other specialists in our field, into a group of people we may not know at all, who may not share any of our expertise. And we'd need to rethink our understanding of the role of social science knowledge in society, too.

It's often important to be able to speak at a high level of abstraction mainly with those who share our particular interests and ways of seeing. But so much of the research we do is too interesting, and too important, to be communicated only with professional scholars—and too important to be left to journalists to translate to nonacademic audiences. To become public scholars, we need to learn how to become translators, too.

When we teach undergraduates, we are actively doing the work of translation, expressing complex ideas in accessible ways. Let's take some of those skills and apply them to the goal of communicating our research to those outside of the classroom. In this age of academic specialization, many of these suggestions will, we hope, also be useful for communicating with scholars outside of your academic discipline.

In this book, we continue some of the conversations that are already taking place across the social sciences about expanding the reach of our scholarship, and we offer practical advice about how to do so. In the following chapters, we'll consider how social scientists can speak beyond the world of specialists, harnessing the power of good writing, along with social media and other new technologies, to make our research an integral part of bigger, bolder discussions about the times in which we live.

Scholars will have different motivations for doing this work. Some of us want to change the world, or at least our little corner of the world. Others wish to make our work more accessible to family members and communities who don't share our expertise—or to colleagues outside of our discipline or scholarly specializations. And certainly the desire for recognition and approval for one's work is often a key consideration, too—we are only human. Regardless of one's motivations, we believe that greater public engagement can enliven public debate and discussion about things that really matter—and also make our scholarly work more incisive.

This is a guidebook for social scientists who wish to engage with broader audiences. The first half of this book mainly focuses on writing; the second half, on using digital media tools. Chapter 1 outlines some basic principles, and dos and don'ts, for writing "beyond the academy." Chapter 2 shows you how to begin to exercise your public voice by writing op-eds and magazine articles, taking you on a step-by-step tour. Chapter 3 looks at books that traverse academic and general audiences, and offers some models of successful general-interest social science books. In chapter 4, we explore the digital tools scholars are using to share their work with wider audiences. In chapter 5, we talk with some scholars about their strategies for building audiences for their work, offering suggestions for how you can do so. Chapter 6 considers the risks entailed in moving your work out into the world, while chapter 7 suggests how you can make public scholarship count, inside and outside of the academy. And now it's time to go public.

... 1 ...

Writing beyond the Academy

Arthur Kleinman, a medical anthropologist who writes about how culture shapes notions of disease and healing, aspires to write prose that is "arresting and beautiful." Most of the time he fails to achieve this, but that does not discourage him, he says. "It is the journey of aspiration that counts, that lets you weigh the best words of strong writers and test them against your own strengths, that lets you experiment, eventually comes to burnish and improve what you do write. And that will matter for your readers and ultimately for the writer in you."[1]

In this age of digital technology, predictions about the demise of the written text, the end of the book, and even the death of the author are commonplace. Nonetheless, writing remains key to communicating. Writing is still the primary way intellectuals win respect for their ideas and influence people. Everyone would prefer to read lively, well-written work. Good writing strives for clarity, energy, and engagement. It is clear, concise, at times personal, and passionate. It conveys its argument economically, and makes the reader want to read what the writer has to say. Rather than simply reporting on research, it engages in a conversation about that research with others.

Writing well is central to learning how to translate your work to broader audiences. In this chapter, we offer four basic principles for creating writing that can participate in lively conversations with varied audiences, not just other academics, but also with nonacademic friends, families, different publics, and even, at times, the people we study—insights culled from our experiences as writers, editors, and teachers of graduate students.

Principle #1: Think of Yourself as a Writer

When we're in graduate school, learning the tools of the academic trade, few of us spend very much time or effort thinking and talking about writing. Many professors assume that students simply know how to write. That may be a fair enough assumption at many elite departments, where students often enter with high levels of cultural capital and solid prior training. Writing is something that comes easily to some people, but for most of us, that isn't true. Good writers aren't born—they're made. Writing is, in other words, a craft that takes learning, and practice. Craftsmen—and women—combine technical skill with imagination and pride in their work.

We tend to imagine a craftsman as a carpenter of sorts, but craftspersons can also be found in the laboratory, concert hall, classroom, and in the study. As artisans, they are dedicated to good work for its own sake—to practical activity—but their labor is not simply a means "to another end," such as career advancement. They are engaged in the fullest way possible with their work and refuse to split their work from the rest of life. A mixture of technique and inspiration, good writing requires an acquaintance with the methodologies of research needed for the task. But there is, C. Wright Mills believed, an unexpected quality about writing too—a "playfulness of mind, as well a truly fierce drive to make sense of the world, which the technician as such usually lacks." The technician wrote Mills, "is too well trained, too precisely trained. Since one can be trained only in what is already known, training sometimes incapacitates one from learning new ways; it makes one rebel against what is bound to be at first loose and even sloppy."

Mills saw writing as a form of self-expression that is as much about the process as the product. A mixture of technique and inspiration, writing is not something that simply happens at the end of the research process. "I am trying to make it damn good all over," Mills wrote of his book *White Collar*. "Simple and clean cut in style, but with a lot of implications and subtleties woven into it. It is my little work of art: it will have to stand for the operations I will never do, not being a surgeon, and for the houses I never built, not being an architect. So you see it has to be a thing of craftsmanship and art as well as science."

Rather than seeing good writing as ornamental at best, or narcissistic or time wasting at worst, we should see it as an integral part of our work, a creative practice that requires practice and dedication, which should have personal meaning for the writer. In this era of academic speedup, as we churn out paper after paper, we rarely pause to craft the elegant phrase. Publishing may stave off one kind of perishing but lead to a less imperceptible but no less insidious kind of wasting: the production of routine work that fails to inspire oneself—or to inspire others. Intellectual craftsmanship, and taking one's writing seriously, can be a mode of resistance. The main reason, Mills said, "I am not alienated is because I write." Writing can make us feel more connected to others, and more connected to the society in which we live.[2]

Principle #2: Know Your Audience

We write for ourselves, to express our ideas and work them out, but we also write for others. And yet, writing guru Helen Sword warns,

"Like lecturers droning on and on in front of classrooms full of dozing students, many academics pay no attention to their audience: They write, but they don't communicate." To write is to raise a claim for the attention of readers, said Mills. Effective writing, in other words, isn't simply an abstract quality—it is about a relationship between a writer and readers. "The skill of writing is to get the reader's circle of meaning to coincide exactly with yours," declared Mills, and "to write in such a way that both of you stand in the same circle of controlled meaning."

The best writers cultivate an authoritative yet conversational voice that bridges the gap between writer and reader. They always sound like human beings. The successful writer, according to Mills, "is a [person] who may shout, whisper, or chuckle, but who is always there." She plays down her erudition instead of scaffolding herself with it. To do so, it is crucial to write with a particular audience in mind; being an effective communicator means knowing your audience. Good writers must develop the knack of putting ourselves in our readers' place, seeing the text through their eyes. If you assume you are a voice, but are not "altogether aware of any public," cautioned Mills, "you may easily fall into unintelligible ravings."

Academics tend to write for a finite group of other experts. Early in graduate school, the audience in your head probably consisted of your professors. For a first book, which often emerges out of a dissertation, you may widen that audience to include particular professors on a tenure committee. Later on, you may imagine an audience comprised of all the experts in your field. If you're writing a journal article, that's fair enough. You should probably write with the editors, reviewers, and readers of that journal in mind.

There are many assumptions built into typical academic writing about what the reader knows in advance—and their willingness to plow through a densely written paper to find out more. While the writing should be persuasive, academics aren't particularly concerned about holding readers' attention. They assume that what they say is inherently interesting, and that their potential readers are sufficiently interested in the topic at hand to read on—even if the writing is less than scintillating.

According to the linguist and psychologist Steven Pinker, the cause of most bad writing is not laziness or sloppiness, but the "curse of knowledge": the writer's inability to put herself in the reader's shoes or to imagine that the reader might not know all that the writer knows—the jargon, the shorthand, the assumptions, the received wisdom. An academic writer is likely to address other experts: the three hundred people who have read everything there is to read about the neoliberal restructuring of higher education, for example. "Lay" audiences are not driven by the same goals, and they do not share the same general background. Because of this, one needs to keep their attention.

Listen to how George Saunders, an award-winning author of non-fiction and short stories, imagines his audience: "I'm essentially trying to impersonate a first-time reader who has to pick up the story and at every point has to decide whether to continue reading. If an intelligent person picks it up, they'll keep going. It's an intimate thing between equals. I'm not above you talking down. We're on the same level. You're just as smart, just as worldly, just as curious as I am."[3]

For many fiction writers and journalists, audiences dictate a great deal. The "Who cares?" and "Why now?" questions determine, to a large extent, what topics they consider important and worthy of attention. Academics think about audience too, but in a very different fashion: they're more likely to write for others who are interested in a particular scholarly literature or substantive issue—other anthropologists of China or experts in public housing policy in social welfare states. Because of their dedication to members of their scholarly tribe, at times they forget how to translate their interest to others—the "curse of knowledge" problem. Or they may have been working on the problem for so long that they've lost a sense of what got them excited about it in the first place.

Sociologist Jodi O'Brien does a helpful little exercise with her graduate students. She has them go around in a circle and tell the group what their dissertation research is about. They inevitably use big words and say something like "the reification of racial distinctions among low-income white and minority youth." Then she asks them what first got them interested in the project. At this point they respond in a very different way, describing their project much more engagingly, expressing the intellectual spark that first captivated them. Instead of examining the "reification of racial distinctions," they're more likely to say something like "how youth understand themselves in relation to racial categories" or "young people's experience of racism." O'Brien's exercise suggests that even though social science research often requires a certain degree of distance, in order to engage in a conversation with nonexperts about the work we do it is important for us to express the spirit of curiosity, excitement, or anger that initially motivated our research and be able to convey it to others.

To speak to multiple audiences, Patricia Hill Collins advises scholars to internalize a sense of having two audiences—our professional peers and those outside of academia—and to maintain contacts in multiple worlds.[4] Let's use our work to "speak truth to power," she says. But let's also "speak truth to the people," taking it to our families and communities, too. To try broadening the audience for your work at least a little bit, envision a group of nonspecialists—your college-educated aunt, your math major friend. Imagine yourself in several different watercooler or dinner party chats. How would you describe your book or article to others? It's difficult to break out of our comfort zones, but the results are often satisfying. Imagine, Mills advised, that you have been asked to give a lecture on some subject you know well, "before an audience of teachers and students from all departments of a leading university as well as an assortment of interested people from a nearby city. Assume that such an audience is before you and that they have a right to know; assume you want to let them know. Now write."[5]

There is a time and a place to converse with our academic peers using the specialized language, theories, methods, and styles of argumentation in our fields. But you can also expand your audience to include your nonacademic friends, community activists, or unknown others. Don't do it out of the goodness of your heart, or because you want to gratify your ego and desire for attention—though of course those motivations always play some role. Do it because it makes your work better. By bringing your research and writing into conversation with those outside the academy, you can test your ideas out and make them stronger. The better you understand your own ideas, the more readily you can articulate them for different audiences.

Principle #3: Strive for Clarity and Concreteness

Complicated ideas sometimes call for complex language. But to the extent that you can, write actively, concisely, and transparently. Use jargon, or specialized language, only when absolutely necessary. "The most powerful ideas in sociology are clearly stated and easily understood," says Sudhir Venkatesh, a sociologist who writes about cities. The notion that nonspecialist writing is simplistic is false. Writing well, and writing for nonspecialist audiences, doesn't have to mean dumbing down your work. In fact, it can mean quite the opposite.

Technical terms are useful if they allow us to state something more precisely than we could otherwise do. But too often we become enamored by what Pierre Bourdieu, quoting Pascal, called "puffed-up" words, for their own sake. (Bourdieu rarely practiced what he preached, however!) Literary critics, and practitioners of interdisciplinary cultural studies, seem to be the worst offenders; historians, the least. Social scientists are somewhere in the middle.

In recent years, the rise of post-structuralist thought, inspired in large part by the writings of Michel Foucault, has had an enormous impact, influencing how we think about such areas as the function of prisons, the nature of mental illness, and the meaning of sexuality. This work is extremely useful at times, and has introduced a host of new insights about modern culture. Yet it has also introduced a whole new stream of jargon, words like "discourses" (systems of thought) and "governmentality" (the practices by which citizens are subjected to governance). In this literature there is a common preference for jargon, and for extra words and clauses that bar entry for those who don't spend a lot of their time steeped in this writing. Certain words that become catchy at particular times can be exceedingly vague.

"Social scientists are expected to use the linguistic symbols of their approach as if they are advertising a brand," laments British sociologist Michael Billig. Are you using jargon to signal to your readers that you are smarter than they are, or to claim membership in an intellectual community? If so, you should think twice about using those terms. Consider whether your intended readers will understand what you're trying to convey if you use them.

Our own experiences as writers, editors, and advisors to graduate students suggest that that authors should use terms such as "neoliberal" or "postmodern" only when they allow us to express something more precisely than we otherwise can. We must be certain that readers will understand what we mean by these terms, and not allow them to substitute for precision or understanding. Don't use the word "resources" when you mean money, or "stakeholders" if you mean people, or "interrelationship" if you mean relationship. Don't use "discourses" when you mean systems of thought, ways of seeing, or modes of speaking. Say people instead of "actors," dominance instead of "hegemony."

Social scientists are known for certain kinds of passive writing: technical phrases that consist overwhelmingly of nouns and noun phrases such as "leadership categorization theory," and passive nominalizations like racialization, or mediatization, which transform people and what they do into things. Nominalization turns verbs into fuzzy nouns. "Investigate" morphs into "investigation"; "applicable" dresses up as "applicability." Check out this description of a course called "Contextualization of Contexts." (We are not making this up.)

> Structure embeds with process and events with networks among observings and signalings, as variously perceived and constituted in levels and extensions. So the central issue is contextualizing contexts wherein social is interdigitated with cultural, narrative with situational.

This is, admittedly, an extreme example, but you get the picture. In order to weed out such nominalizations, scan manuscripts for words that end in -tion, -ism, -ty, -ment, -ness, -ance, and -ence. Avoid these words wherever possible. Then grab a more active verb and slip in a concrete noun (when it makes the sentence better). Find a more concrete way of describing what exactly is happening when someone is doing some "reifying"!

Some versions of sociology describe and analyze broad structures, forces, and social formations, leaving out the flesh and blood players, the people who exist within the structures, who create social life. Describing structural changes without actors, contexts that are not peopled, does not make for very engaging storytelling, however. While such writing may at times be acceptable to publish in academic journals—though even there, they should be avoided—passive sentences make writing less engaging, less energetic, and more timid. Passive writing and wordiness typically go together, and result in a lack of clarity. Don't use several words when fewer would do. See, for example, the handy dandy list compiled by the blog *Shit Academics Say*, which contrasts "inflated" and "concise" writing (text box 1.1).

As you can see from this list, concise writing flows better and is less pedantic than inflated, cluttered writing. It is also less likely to lead to the cardinal sin of academic writing: passive voice. Clutter muddies a sentence's meaning by driving nouns and verbs apart, creating passive sentences.

Text Box 1.1 The Busy Academic's Guide to Writing Concisely

Inflated		Concise
along the lines of	shorten to	like
as a matter of fact	shorten to	in fact
at all times	shorten to	always
at the present time	shorten to	now, currently
at this present time	shorten to	now, currently
because of the fact that	shorten to	because
by means of	shorten to	by
draw your attention	shorten to	point out
due to the fact that	shorten to	because
for the purpose of	shorten to	for
for the reason that	shorten to	because
have the ability to	shorten to	be able to, can
in light of the fact that	shorten to	because
in order to	shorten to	to
in regards to	shorten to	on, about
in spite of the fact that	shorten to	although, though
in the event that	shorten to	if
in the final analysis	shorten to	finally
in the nature of	shorten to	like
in the neighborhood of	shorten to	about
make decisions about	shorten to	decide on
on the occasion of	shorten to	when
on two separate occasions	shorten to	twice
the level of water rose	shorten to	the water rose
the majority of	shorten to	most
the people who are located in	shorten to	the people in
the pie that is included in	shorten to	the pie in
until such time as	shorten to	until
with reference to	shorten to	of, on, for, about

Source: *Shit Academics Say*, https://mobile.twitter.com/AcademicsSay.

Learn to identify passive verb forms: a form of the verb "to be" paired with the past participle of the main verb (as in sentences such as "taxes were raised"). People often use passive voice to avoid using the first-person pronoun "I." But the passive voice slows down your writing, sounds unnatural, and robs verbs of impact. Compare another example: "The data was analyzed," or "I analyzed the data." Which one says more about who did what? Clearly, the second example does. Another clue to passive voice is the habit of beginning sentences with a nonspecific pronoun "it." Consider, for example, these sentences: "It was believed that in two short years . . ." or "It was commonly believed . . ." In both cases, the pronoun "it" lacks a clear referent. These sentences not only commit acts of passive voice—they are also just plain vague.

Clear subjects and active verbs help readers understand the relationships between people and events, provide variety, and add punch. Passive sentences, in contrast, have no clearly defined agent or action. They can't answer the question "who's kicking whom?" Passive sentences are often signaled by a "be" verb plus a past tense verb: "are signaled," "can be shown," "is affected." If you're still not clear on when you are using the passive voice, try putting the phrase "by zombies" at the end of the sentence. If it makes sense, you've written a sentence in the passive voice. For example, take the sentence: "The lamp was broken." Does it make sense if "by zombies" is placed at the end? If the answer is yes, you've used a passive voice.

Excessive use of nouns versus verbs, the overuse of abstract nouns (application, theory, discourse, trajectory, evidence, process), and the overuse of abstract verbs (be, apply, consider, correlate, are, been) lead to passive sentences. Here's an example of a sentence that is hampered by abstract nouns and passive phrasing:

Despite this grassroots activism, and even as food and agriculture gain increasing prominence in media and policy circles, maintaining an emphasis upon the kinds of inequalities these activists work to dismantle remains important and challenging work.

This is an excerpt from an article that describes and analyzes a compelling phenomenon: the struggle for food justice in low-income neighborhoods. But it is filled with vague statements that detract from its immediacy. One of the culprits here is the phrase "maintaining an emphasis upon." Substitute "emphasizing" for this wordy phrase, and you say the same thing using fewer words. It sounds better, and you establish a clearer connection between the subject (activists) and what they're doing (trying to dismantle inequalities). "Remains" is a weak verb, for which we should substitute "is." Once we do that, consider this:

> Despite this grassroots activism, even as food and agriculture gain increasing prominence in media and policy circles, challenging inequalities is important and challenging work.

While this is still less than a perfectly constructed sentence, we think you will agree that it sounds a whole lot better than it did before, and doesn't lose anything in the process. Here's another example of a wordy, passive sentence from that same essay:

> Another example often referenced by food justice activists is the discrimination faced by farmers of color at the hands of the United States Department of Agriculture.

There are far better ways to begin a sentence than with the phrase "another example." The author above sounds like she is just going through the motions, and reporting rather than communicating with her readers. "Referenced" is also a weak verb, one that should be jettisoned. And rather than speak of "discrimination faced by farmers of color," let's phrase the sentence more actively, to read as follows:

Food justice activists often speak of how the United States Department of Agriculture discriminates against farmers of color.

This sentence sounds much more vital and active. There is a clear connection between the doers (food justice activists) and what they're up to (charging the USDA with discriminating against them). This sentence ends, as it should, with its most important part—the claim of discrimination against farmers of color.

The moral of this story is crystal clear: write as concisely as you can. Brevity truly is the soul of wit. Then rewrite. Edit yourself. If you have trouble doing so, have others edit your work. Excise unnecessary wordiness, and turn passive into active sentences. A sentence almost always sounds better if you use fewer words. Cutting back your prose, like pruning a beautiful rosebush, can allow the vitality, precision, and emotional heart of a piece of writing to emerge.

Communicating transparently, rather than scaffolding ourselves with lots of citations, tables, and other demonstrations of rigor, may expose weaknesses in our thinking. Once we've become socialized into academic modes of writing, shedding the armor of jargon, footnotes, and other professional conventions can make us feel exceedingly vulnerable. We are afraid of exposing ourselves. Do we lose something if we say something simply? It can make us feel naked; our ideas are out there with nothing to stand between them and the reader. Writing more transparently, rather than arming ourselves with lots of citations, can force us to make an argument we may feel tentative about.

Lack of clarity can be a smokescreen, a way of equivocating. Own your words, and your ideas. If you know what you're talking about, you can safely energize your prose with active words. Describe as vividly as you can, but also offer an explanation of why something is occurring, why now, and who and what is producing it. Use literature selectively, to situate your work in a larger conversation, not to hide behind the work of others.

Write sentences that are concise, verb-driven, and filled with concrete details. Use plenty of active, specific, concrete nouns and vivid verbs, especially when discussing abstract concepts. Keep nouns and verbs close together, so that readers can identify who's kicking whom. Pay attention to the difference between precision and mealy-mouthed qualification. Be careful using "might," "should," "often," "would seem," "perhaps," and other phrases that mitigate your claims. Excessive qualification makes you look timid and your argument halfhearted.

Finally, be mindful of the rhythm of your writing. Vary the length of your sentences. Avoid long uninterrupted paragraphs made up of endless sentences, filled with compound thoughts and phrases. Try reading your prose out loud. Clunky sentences sound a whole lot clunkier when you're forced to listen to them. Try to hear the cadence and rhythm of the prose. Use contractions ("can't" for "can not," "won't" for "will not") where they feel right. For many authors, and for an accessible style, contractions are appropriate; but some prose contractions can feel forced. Be adaptable, but err on the side of the less formal. Think of the words you use and make every word matter.

By using verbs that describe what people are actually doing we make our writing less passive, more elegant, and more precise. They also give the actors we are describing more "agency." By peopling our prose, rather than filling it with objects, we embody through our writing the belief that social change is possible. "A world composed of big, impersonal things," writes Michael Billig, "will appear unmoveable, as compared with people who can be identified, praised, blamed and even changed."[6] Passive writing helps produce a vision of the social world that is alienated and alienating. Vivid language, in contrast, describes real people interacting with their world.

Principle #4: Show and Tell

The philosopher and psychologist William James once said that all human thought is essentially of two kinds: narrative, descriptive, and contemplative thought, on one hand; and reasoning, on the other. These correspond roughly to two different kinds of storytelling—showing and telling—and two different groups of professional storytellers. If journalists are trained to "show—not tell," social scientists are mainly concerned with telling: describing large patterns of events and explaining why those events may be occurring. We believe that there is something beyond the surface of social life: structures, routines, ideas that make the world go round. Rather than simply recounting details of an event, a life, a social problem, we offer interpretations, answering the why questions. Rather than leave it to the author to make sense of material, we like to tell people how to think about it.

But the best scholarly writers also engage their readers' love of stories. Sarah Thornton is a sociologist who writes popular books about the art world that are richly descriptive. "I want my writing to be educational but also entertaining," she says. She aspires to research like an academic but write like a reporter, she says. "I think that people remember narratives better than expositions. If you ask someone in the street to tell you oh, that story they heard yesterday or that argument they heard yesterday, they remember the story better than the argument."[7]

Storytelling is deeply ingrained in human behavior. We see evidence of this everywhere: from little children who plead, "tell me a story" before going to sleep, to the recent boom in podcasting, such as This American Life. Human beings are a storytelling species. By telling stories, we construct meaning out of the seemingly random events of our lives. Human time is lived through our stories and personal narratives that connect events that unfold through time, where characters interact with one another in different settings. We all look for "core human drama, whether that is suffering or some form of triumph," according to Arthur Frank, who writes about the kinds of stories that people tell about illness. Action is dramatic, he reminds us, "when something is at stake."[8]

The classic narrative arc structures most of the stories that surround us, in literature, television, or theater. It begins with exposition, with setting the stage, and then leads to rising action, which results in a climax, and is then followed by further action, and then a resolution. In contrast, the academic's narrative arc is far less linear, taking into account every conceivable variable that may disprove one's thesis. It goes something like this: exposition, description of data, more exposition, and then even more data (the climax!), and then moves on to findings, conclusions, a series of caveats about the limitations of one's data, the difficulty of generalizing, and a plea for "further research."

By accounting for and recognizing all the various complexities of human existence, you can overwhelm and lose your audience.[9] Academics who wish to make their work more engaging must find a narrative arc that can transform a complex argument into a story that can draw nonexperts in. This requires showing and telling, painting a portrait of a group, a scene, or a trend that unfolds over time, offering thick description while analyzing what is occurring beneath the surface of events. The best journalists know how to do this well. But others can use these techniques too.

Journalists know how to paint a portrait of the here and now, the immediate and novel. A journalistic story tends to have a central figure that guides the narrative, and it is usually someone the intended audience can relate to. In order to hook a reader, they must tell a story through the eyes of a character that readers can identify with. When journalists tell stories about social phenomena, such as hooking up on college campuses and other social trends, they tend to tell them through the lives of individuals—they show the reader what is going on, painting portraits of scenes and characters.

In his award-winning magazine essay "The Case for Reparations," Ta-Nehisi Coates tells the story of Clyde Ross and his experience of housing segregation. Coates knew that he had to "hook" readers with a personal narrative in order to tell the story of systemic racism in US housing policy, a complex subject that would probably be boring to most readers. If he hadn't placed a compelling personal story at the center of his narrative, chances are that Coates would fail to engage many readers; fewer people would know or be persuaded by his case for reparations.[10] One method of reaching broader audiences, according to Cheryl Brumley, who advises social scientists at the London School of Economics, is to focus on the smaller picture:

> You must accept that details important to you, and to your colleagues, may not resonate with other people. Is there anything in your research that may, though? When considering this question, be honest with yourself, and try to embody someone else who hasn't spent years toiling over your niche subject area. You know, someone like any one of those other seven billion people on the planet. Once you find that potential point of connection, use it to hammer home a specific and illustrative point.

For example, Brumley worked on a podcast with a professor of history and philosophy, Mary Morgan, who tracks how economics went from a discipline based on words to one based on mathematical models. Instead of trying to summarize Morgan's research in a ten-minute podcast sequence, she made the idea of economic modeling more accessible to readers by relating it to a woman weighing options between sex and murder. As Brumley advises, "Resist the temptation of covering too much of your research. Don't get bogged down in the details. Find that central image that people can connect with."[11]

Unlike journalists, who have to hook a reader and keep them reading, for academics, whether and how people read their work is disconnected from their professional success. The sheer fact of publication leads to hiring and promotion. If the work is well received after it's published, well, that's icing on the cake. As social scientists become socialized into the profession, we follow tried-and-true writing formulas, exemplified by the standard journal article: abstract, literature review, methodological discussion, findings, and conclusion. This structure offers us a template, and may give us confidence to share our ideas. This format may be well suited for writing for those we know fairly well—other specialists knowledgeable about social stratification or the epistemology of science—but to nonspecialists, it's not all that appealing. Conforming to this model can speed one's academic productivity, but it rarely generates very inspired writing, sadly.

An overriding focus on analytical rigor can lead to writing that lacks energy and engagement, that is passive, and even timid. It can lead us to fear making claims that we cannot fully substantiate. It makes our work measured and sober, but also leads to intellectual conservatism and a reticence to push into unfamiliar territory. Putting one's ideas out there boldly can seem risky, to be sure.

Yet social scientists are, in essence, storytellers. We tell stories about societies using numbers if we are quantitative sociologists. We use vignettes and descriptive or novelistic techniques if we are ethnographers. We use social-historical methods to tell stories about societies through time. We are centrally engaged with studying essential human dramas: making a living, falling in love, engaging in social conflicts. When we write, we need to convey that passion and surprise, a sense of having revealed something that is counterintuitive, an idea that clashes with the conventional wisdom. Instead, we too often simply "write up" our research results.

"To overcome the 'academic prose,'" Mills famously wrote, "you have first to overcome the academic pose." Begin by reading widely: nonacademic books, novels, academic books, articles out of one's fields of interest, magazines, and blogs. Figure out the sort of writing that inspires you and that you would like to emulate. Equipped with the belief that you are in fact a writer who wishes to communicate with varied audiences, try telling a story about your research, a story that might appeal both to your academic colleagues and to your Aunt Sally. Sally may not know what your discipline is all about, but she is curious enough to try to find out—perhaps because she wants to understand what you, her niece the sociologist, is up to. Write for her. And start small.

... **2** ...

Telling Stories about Your Research

Perhaps you have just completed a book manuscript on the motivations of individuals who take part in random acts of mass violence. A shooting occurs in a high school somewhere in Middle America, and you feel that you have a new way of understanding why these tragedies occur, or an explanation that goes beyond the newspaper headlines. That's a perfect time to pitch an op-ed to a newspaper, write a short feature for a digital magazine, or perhaps write a long-form narrative about your research. By doing so, you can try to influence the public discussion of something you're passionately interested in and knowledgeable about.

Or maybe you've got an idea for a story that is based on a research project you've participated in, which you'd like to share with a larger audience, but you don't have a book in mind. Consider writing a shorter piece, for an online news magazine, about your research. In this chapter, we look at newspaper op-eds, online news websites, and long-form magazines as potential outlets for your work. We describe the different requirements for writing in these venues and offer close-up looks at articles that use journalistic techniques to tell a story about social research. Writing shorter pieces can help you develop your public voice, and an audience for your work.

One format academics utilize to tell a story about their research to nonacademic publics is the op-ed, or "opinion-editorial," in a local or national newspaper. Op-eds are typically short and opinionated, as the name suggests. They concern themselves with a subject of broad appeal, something that is "newsworthy," which typically means recently in the news. When an event related to your research hits the news cycle, it's good to have 750 words on the topic so that you can connect it to the "news peg," or current event. This is what the *New York Times* op-ed editor advises for prospective op-ed contributors to that venerable newspaper:

> Most pieces we publish are between 400 and 1200 words. They can be longer when they arrive, but not so long that they're traumatizing. Submissions that are reacting to news of the world are of great value to us, especially if they arrive very quickly. Write in your own voice. If you're funny, be funny. Don't write the way you think important people write, or the way you think important pieces should sound. And it's best to focus very specifically on something; if you write about the general problem of prisons in the United States, the odds are that it will seem too familiar. But if you are a prisoner in California and you have just gone on a hunger strike and you want to tell us about it—now, that we would like to read. We are normal humans (relatively speaking). We like to read conversational English that pulls us along. That means that if an article is written with lots of jargon, we probably won't like it.[1]

Now, chances are that few scholars will have prison experience (though there may in fact be some who do), but those who study prisons will have expertise about prison life to share with others. Having experience and expertise about something is not necessarily sufficient to publish an op-ed: you need to comment on something that is currently in the news. In writing an op-ed, ask yourself, what is the news hook for the piece I want to pitch? If you are pitching an op-ed to an editor, they will want to know that the piece you're going to write for them is timely and relates to the news cycle they operate within. (For more on this, see chapter 4.)

In writing a short piece about a complex subject, structure is key; there is a formula, more or less, for op-ed writing. We quote Dalton Conley, a sociologist who occasionally contributes to the pages of the *New York Times* and other publications, at length on this. (See his very useful "Op-Ed Tip Sheet" for more specific advice.)

> The first graph has four or five lines. The first line mentions the
> peg. The second line sets up the "fight." The third line intimates
> the argument—that you know something these other folks don't.
> And the fourth line previews your recommendation based on your
> secret knowledge. . . . The next three or so paragraphs then start
> fresh and explain the background of the problem; tip your hat at
> the opposition; and lead the reader through your counter-intuitive,
> yet brilliant, logic. . . . Then in the penultimate graph, you need to
> inoculate yourself against your enemies (and believe me, any Op-Ed
> worth reading will garner you enemies, no matter how obscure the
> issue may appear). . . . In the final paragraph, you will come back to
> your argument and get a bit more specific about your recommenda-
> tion. . . . And then, you will circle back to the specific peg . . . with
> some wise line at the very end. . . . That's the formula.[2]

While such formulas should not be followed slavishly, they can give you a place to begin. But in fact, when Ruth Milkman, a sociologist, published an op-ed in the *New York Times* on the state of organized labor, it departed from this model but was nonetheless successful. Here's what she wrote:

> It is a time of trial for organized labor. Only 13 percent of nonagri-
> cultural workers are unionized. The figure is even lower among

immigrants who toil at unskilled jobs in the nation's newest industries. Employers have abandoned the paternalistic job security measures, pensions and fringe benefits of which they boasted only a few years ago. Instead, they are imposing wage cuts and speedups on their workers while the American Federation of Labor stands by helplessly.

Sound familiar? This was the labor movement's plight in 1935. Like many Americans today, people back then believed that labor unions had become weak and irrelevant. In 1932, George Barnett, president of the American Economics Association, declared, "American trade unionism is slowly being limited in influence by changes which destroy the basis on which it is erected." Yet a few years later, the Congress of Industrial Organizations, an insurgent group within organized labor born out of a debate that few outsiders bothered to follow, set off America's greatest surge of unionism. That growth continued, peaking at 35 percent of the workforce just before the two rival labor federations reunited in 1955, forming today's A.F.L.-C.I.O.

In the first two paragraphs, the author sets up her argument about the reasons for the decline of organized labor in the contemporary United States. By using the historical example in the first paragraph, and comparing it to the current context, she gets our attention, and shows us that we've been hearing about the decline of organized labor for over half a century. Then, in the next paragraph, she tells us that the state of organized labor has worsened even further recently.

Now the unionization rate has sunk to about 8 percent of all private-sector non-farm workers. Globalization and the service economy have displaced the mass production industries that produced the last great internal union upheaval 70 years ago. Those industries, and the New Deal legal and political order that the C.I.O. helped shape, have been weakened beyond recognition.

The news peg comes in the fourth paragraph: a plan by a dissident union leader to merge industry unions. Is this the solution to organized labor's woes? Milkman thinks it is.

> Next month, at the A.F.L.-C.I.O. annual convention in Chicago, a sharpening dispute over how labor should meet these challenges will reach a turning point. A dissident group led by Andy Stern, who heads the 1.8 million–member Service Employees International Union (the A.F.L.-C.I.O.'s largest affiliate), is trying to oust John Sweeney, the federation's president, and engineer a major shift in organized labor's strategy. Outspoken and impatient, Mr. Stern has angered his colleagues in union circles by threatening to pull his union out of the A.F.L.-C.I.O. if his reform program is not adopted. But for all his abrasiveness, his program offers labor's best hope— maybe its only hope—for revitalization.

She then offers an explanation of why she thinks the proposed consolidation is promising, who supports it, and who doesn't.

> Mr. Stern's Change to Win program calls for a one-union-per-industry model that would curb competition among unions and increase the organizing capacity of those that remain. Changing job descriptions have rendered many traditional union jurisdictions obsolete, so that unions often end up competing against one another for members. Merging industry unions would also make it harder for employers to play off one union against another.
>
> Consider the airline industry: at least five unions represent pilots, three represent flight attendants and six represent ground crews and ticket agents. This balkanization has made it harder for unions to fight assaults on their livelihood by companies like United Airlines, which recently shed its pension obligations, opening the door for other airlines to threaten their workers with the same fate. Today, federal, state and local government employees are scattered among 13 unions, and health care workers among more than . . .

The proposed consolidation of the A.F.L.-C.I.O.'s 58 affiliates threatens many vested interests, not least those of the officials who head smaller unions. But a handful of the largest unions—the Teamsters, Laborers, Unite Here and United Food and Commercial Workers—have embraced Mr. Stern's reform agenda. These unions make up 40 percent of the A.F.L.-C.I.O.'s membership, and may join the service employees union in bolting from the federation if they lose their bid to transform it.

Milkman supports the insurgents' proposed consolidation effort because it promises to do what she, an expert on labor and labor history, thinks is needed: boost spending to organize unorganized workers.

The insurgents have also called for spending $60 million—about half the federation's budget—on organizing, versus the $22.5 million that Mr. Sweeney has offered. They argue that if labor is going to survive, its most urgent priority must be increasing the percentage of unionized Americans. But only a few A.F.L.-C.I.O. unions—most of them Mr. Stern's allies—have put more money and effort into organizing.

Ten years ago, Mr. Sweeney—who was Mr. Stern's predecessor as the service employees union president and his onetime mentor—was elected to the A.F.L.-C.I.O. presidency on a platform of "organizing the unorganized." But because he presides over a federation of unions whose current structure does not allow him to enforce his will, Mr. Sweeney has been unable to reverse the tide of union decline. That's why another key plank in the Change to Win platform is to strengthen the power of the central federation itself.

Having clearly articulated the different positions of Sweeney and Stern, and argued in favor of Stern, Milkman offers additional evidence for why she believes in Stern's superiority: his track record as a leader of a service employees union is the best fit for today's labor force, concentrated as it is in service work. She also uses her expertise to point to where she thinks the future of organized labor lies: orga-nizing the unorganized, and confronting the impact of globalization.

> The service employees union's track record is the best case for tak-ing its proposal seriously: it has tripled in size over the past quarter-century, as membership in most other unions plunged. It is on the front lines of the nation's service-based economy, the leading edge of the race to the bottom that threatens to drag down labor stan-dards for the rest of us. And with an eye on globalization's impact, its building service division has formed alliances with unions overseas to advance its organizing in the United States, where janitors and security guards are often employed by foreign-owned companies that offer workers in their home countries better pay and working conditions.

To conclude, the author references the historical anecdote she led with, effectively driving her main point home, making a specific rec-ommendation.[3]

> With unions in decline, real wages for hourly workers are stagnant, their health and pension benefits are in tatters, and inequalities between rich and poor have widened to levels not seen since the 1920's and early 1930's—just before the last great union surge. Given a chance, Mr. Stern's proposals can restore labor as the coun-terforce it once was in an era that saw remarkable gains in prosper-ity for all Americans.[4]

Milkman's op-ed is an example of how scholars can use their exper-tise to offer insight into a pressing social issue, such as the fate of labor unions, by commenting on something in the news: in this case, a union election that portends a major alignment of power and pri-orities. What is at stake in this election? Milkman uses a historical comparison to anchor her claim about the future of labor and offers a bite-sized analysis of the challenges facing labor unions today to support her argument that an insurgent leader offers a ray of hope at a time of shrinking unionization. It's an example of how social scientists can deepen journalistic analysis and offer an opinionated take on current events. But don't let news cycles dictate your forays into public scholarship, particularly in the digital era, when there are many more possible venues for your work.

Digital Magazines

The rise of digital media means that many traditional magazines and newspapers also distribute content online, supplementing the articles that appear in print with blog posts from freelance authors. As newspapers (regrettably) cut back staff positions, they are increasingly relying upon freelancers, including academics, to fill their pages. Tressie McMillan Cottom does research on for-profit colleges. While it's not a topic that is regularly covered in the news, developments in higher education are at times newsworthy. Cottom drafted an op-ed on the subject of her research. When the *New York Times* ran a "Room for Debate" column on financial aid, she pitched her piece and it was published. By writing in this condensed form about her research for the *Times*, Cottom built an audience for a future, longer-length piece. (For more on this, see chapter 5, "Building an Audience.")

Sociologist Jennifer Lena published a seventeen-hundred-word piece in *Pacific Standard*, a politics and current affairs online magazine, about her research. In "Why Hipsters Hate on Lana Del Rey," she explores the questions, "Why *do* music fans obsess about authenticity? What's at stake when a fan argues, with emotions riding high, that Taylor Swift is too pop to be country, or that Green Day isn't authentic punk rock?"[5] Drawing upon extensive research, Lena makes debates about authenticity in music come alive by telling a story about her research, and by commenting on music videos from the likes of rappers Sugar Hill Gang and Jay-Z, along with Del Rey. It's showing and telling (and listening) at its best.[6]

Today, many magazines look less like the paper glossies you browse at the dentist's office and more like swipe-able, download-able apps on mobile digital devices. Some have print counterparts that charge for subscriptions; many do not. These are great places for academics to publish in. If you have trouble placing your op-ed in a print venue—or even if you don't—you might try instead any number of online news and entertainment websites, such as *Salon*, *Pacific Standard*, or *Huffington Post*, which are always looking for fresh "content," and can sometimes accommodate longer-length pieces. Pitching a topic that is in the news helps, though it's not always a requirement. And if a piece is particularly timely and well crafted, chances are it will be reposted elsewhere.

Sociologist Paul Hirschfield has long been interested in the issue of police brutality. "My passions were regularly inflamed by incidents such as police shootings of unarmed people that led to no meaningful consequences," he said. Recently, in the wake of a number of high-profile police shootings, he found himself devoting more and more of his spare time to posting, commenting on, and debating such incidents on Facebook. "Although my actions were mostly driven by a sense of anger and a desire to see some justice done," he said, "I also saw this as an opportunity to educate my Facebook friends and, by extension, some of their friends, as well as total strangers, about this complex issue."[7]

His Facebook posts were sociologically informed and compelling enough to draw the attention of the editor of *Sociological Forum*, who asked him to contribute an essay on police violence in the United States. Data confirming that rates of deadly police violence were much higher in the United States than in other industrialized countries had recently been compiled. In the meantime, a close friend remarked that it was a shame that his posts about policing issues were seen only by his limited social circle on Facebook. "I agreed that this was not a very effective use of my activist or intellectual energies," Hirschfield says. "So I wrote an op-ed that synthesized many of the points I had been making in on-line forums. The gist of the piece was that current laws are designed to protect police rather than the public. The public deserves (and presumably prefers) laws that strike a more even balance between police safety and public safety."

The piece was rejected by every major publication he sent it to, including the *New York Times*, *Slate*, *Salon*, *Huffington Post*, and *Newsweek*. They told him it was too long, so he kept cutting and refining it. But having tired of dealing with nonresponsive editors, he pitched the piece to *The Conversation*, an online news source that specializes in publishing scholars' research (tagline: "Academic Rigor, Journalistic Flair"), which immediately accepted it, publishing it to coincide with the now predictable release of yet another tragic video of the murder of a black person by a police officer.[8] That morning, Hirschfield's article was picked up by RawStory, and soon after by *Newsweek* and then by *Huffington Post*. *Newsweek* and *Huffington Post* eventually published the op-ed, despite the fact that they had earlier rejected it. With help from countless other outlets, the piece received at least ninety-five thousand views as of this writing, including fifteen thousand on an Indian website.

What Hirschfield's experience suggests is that good timing is extremely important; the fact that his story coincided with a major news event helped it go "viral." His success also suggests that pitching your work to an online publication such as *The Conversation*, which is attuned to both the academic and journalistic worlds, can be a far better use of your time than spending a great deal of effort trying to score a slot on the *New York Times'* sought-after opinion pages—or *Newsweek's*. Eventually, it may end up there anyway.

Sometimes authors who are committed to writing a particular piece simply write the thing, and then shop it around until they get someone to publish it. (Sending the same piece to more than one publication at a time is verboten, however.) It's usually a good idea to query an editor first, to see if they're interested, before you go ahead and write about a particular subject. To interest an editor in your work, you will need to send them a "pitch." (Your university public affairs office, if you have one, may also be willing to submit an op-ed on your behalf.) Pitching to an editor involves researching the style and focus of the publication, and then contacting the editor with your idea about a piece that would be timely and appeal to readers. The pitch, which ranges from one to two single-spaced pages, should be engagingly written and give the editor (whom you should address personally) a clear sense of what you will write, a demonstration of your writing chops, and your qualifications. It should present a capsule version of your argument, and explain why it's important now.

End the pitch with a paragraph that offers a brief introduction to your work, such as "I am a sociologist who has published four award-winning books about the environment and climate change." If you have a website, provide a link so that they can peruse it. Editors don't have time to respond to every query, particularly when it's from someone they haven't worked with in the past, so you may need to nudge an editor and then back off. But persistence—along with good writing and powerful storytelling—can often pay off.

The Long-Form Article

Longer magazine pieces in magazines such as *Harper's*, the *New Yorker*, or the *Atlantic* entail reporting—talking to actual people— to tell a story. These pieces tend to be "greenlit" by editors who read and approve pitches by staff writers and freelancers. They appeal to those who prefer a more luxurious thirty-five hundred to five thousand words to make an argument. Since editors tend to work with writers they already have relationships with, who are likely to be experienced journalists, it is often difficult for academics to break into these outlets. Being a talented prose stylist certainly helps.

In order to interest readers in a subject and inspire them to read on, feature articles need a compelling narrative, or story. Stories tend to have two essential building blocks: characters and scenes. Many of us like to read about people. We like to read about lives that we can identify with or that seem very different than our own. In our articles and books, social scientists tend to show people who are born at a certain time and in a certain place, surrounded by carefully selected contexts, but who are rarely *doing* anything. Rather than simply reporting on your research, try to tell a story through characters, showing how individuals, and the groups they are part of, change over time. Individuals may be held back by their circumstances—such as economic constraints or the cultural expectations that surround them—but chances are that they are trying to resist those constraints and create a decent life for themselves and those they care about. Show us characters who develop over time, who are driven by some set of needs, desires, or aspirations. What challenges do the individuals or groups you're studying face, and how do they address them?

Try to provide a sense of place, too, offering insight into how the characters you are writing about inhabit particular settings. In much social science work, while place is extremely important, it is often downplayed as a factor influencing social events. For example, even in this era of globalization, when messages are carried at lightning speed on the Internet, social movements tend to mobilize in particular places. An urban park became the scene for the extraordinary protests against economic concentration that became known as Occupy Wall Street. When ACT-UP activists mobilized in cities across the nation to fight the AIDS crisis, different local organizations were shaped by the distinctive histories of the cities they were in. Even though we are in the business of making social scientific generalizations, we should seize upon opportunities to paint vivid snapshots of action that takes place in particular contexts.

In narrative terms, a scene consists of things happening to people in a particular place. Long-form narratives are typically comprised of several scenes, which are settings for dramatic action. As your subjects move through time, they're doing something—raising children, engaging in conflicts, working, making relationships, growing, and dying. They're doing so as individuals, but also in relation to the people they're closest to: family members, friends, workmates, or members of the communities or organizations they are a part of. Why not try to convey some of the quotidian texture of their lives, how they change, and what conflicts engage, and change them?

To write a feature article about your work, borrow journalistic techniques and some conventions of magazine writing. Channel the spirit of C. Wright Mills and share a little story about a big issue that shows and tells. Convey a sense of the color, movement and texture of everyday and exceptional moments, to make an argument about something people care about. One effective strategy of storytelling is to take the reader on your research excursion, introducing her to your research subjects and reflecting upon them, how they see the world, and what they tell us about the subject you're studying. Don't settle for cardboard characters who remain fixed and one-dimensional. Try, instead, through description, dialogue, and dramatic tension, to capture complexity, contradiction, and ambivalence and to convey a sense of emotional depth.

A few publications publish hybrids of social science and journalistic writing. *Contexts* magazine, sponsored by the American Sociological Association, is one of them. It seeks to make cutting-edge social research accessible to general readers as well as social researchers. Situated in an academic discipline but speaking beyond it, *Contexts* engages professional sociologists who value the opportunity to read about new research, to find out what their colleagues are doing. It is also read by students of sociology, both savvy undergraduate and graduate students—and, at times, by your Aunt Sally, too.

To write for a hybrid publication such as *Contexts*, you must tell a good story and populate it with living, breathing human beings. Particularize an idea in a way that doesn't oversimplify. Focus on people, places, and moments, to illuminate larger processes. The story has to be big enough to captivate sociological interest. That is, it should deal with a theme that is of general interest but which is also specific enough to be compelling. Try to engage the attention of a general reader—a challenging feat in an age where Internet, blogs, social media, and so many other things are competing for our attention. If academic journals publish articles in which authors "tell," or report on their findings, and magazine writing requires authors to "show"—to describe, set scenes, and allow interviewees to speak— *Contexts'* hybrid style asks you to show *and* tell. It shifts the understanding of who the audience is, calling upon authors to connect the story to some big ideas, articulating an angle that defies conventional wisdom.

An article should have an idea, or thesis, rather than simply be about a particular topic. Don't write about the declining educational quality of state universities—that's too general. A good story needs a clear argument or angle. Tell the story of state universities by focusing, more narrowly, on one group of people and their experiences. A good idea has specificity, a distinctive angle, and is timely, fresh. It advances the conversation, challenges the conventional wisdom, and answers the proverbial "so what" question. Let's look at one successful feature article and how it achieves this.

A Story of Class, Gender, and Education

A while back, *Contexts* published an article entitled "The (Mis)Education of Monica and Karen," written by sociologists Laura Hamilton and Elizabeth Armstrong. They based the article on their research about how working-class students, particularly women, fare at large flagship state universities—such as one they studied for five years in the Midwest.[9] It is also about the fate of universities in an age of growing commercialization. Following a dormitory floor of female students through their college careers and into the workforce, the study featured interviews with students and their parents. What they found was intriguing—and disturbing. While these young women had achieved well enough in high school to gain admittance to their flagship state university, once they got there they were not well served by that institution.

One of the things that makes "The (Mis)Education of Monica and

Karen" a strong piece is that it illuminates the big story of shifting priorities of state education to show how it is affecting one group of students: working-class young women. A story about working-class women at one university would be too narrow. A story about working-class students at state universities would be too broad to be engaging. Here we have a story about working-class young women that analyzes broader trends in public education. The article doesn't just make an argument—it tells a story that provides a window into the lives of these young women.

How do Hamilton and Armstrong accomplish this feat? First, in this world of fading attention spans and increasing competition for attention, the title (which is, in this case, a riff on a Lauryn Hill album) draws the reader in, piquing his or her interest and telling the reader a bit about what the article is about. Then, beginning in the first paragraph, the authors set the scene, introducing us to a young woman they call Monica.

> Monica grew up in a small, struggling Midwestern community, population 3,000, that was once a booming factory town. She was from a working-class family, and paid for most of her education at Midwest U, a "moderately selective" residential university, herself. She worked two jobs, sometimes over 40 hours a week, to afford in-state tuition. Going out of state, or to a pricey private school, was simply out of the question without a large scholarship. Attending MU was even a stretch; one year there cost as much as four years at the regional campus near her hometown.

Popular writers know that it is important to grab the reader with a compelling title and an intriguing introduction. The importance of the lead, or introductory sentences, cannot be overstated. The first few paragraphs draw the reader in, setting the scene for the rest of the story with a brief opening vignette. It offers a "hook" that captures the reader's interest and tells us why the story is relevant now—something that is of broad public interest, or a current controversy. Your hook answers the "why" question, and tells a reader why they're reading your story right now. In this particular story, the first paragraph suggests that it is important because it illuminates the experiences of working-class students at large state universities and some of the struggles they face.

The next two paragraphs begin to develop the angle, or the thesis, that will be further expanded upon in the rest of the article. The second paragraph moves the story forward, introducing Karen, the other main character in the article:

> Karen grew up in the same small town as Monica, but in a solidly middle class family. Her college-educated parents could afford to provide more financial assistance. But even though MU was only three hours away, her father "wasn't too thrilled" about her going so far from home. He had attended a small religious school that was only 10 minutes away.

Through this comparison, we began to understand that this is going to be a story about how class background shapes educational experiences at MU. We're intrigued by the vignettes—hopefully!—but we're still not entirely clear about what the article is about. Then, in the third paragraph, which contains what journalists call the "nutgraf" (really the thesis of the article), the authors shift into telling mode:

> Karen and Monica's stories offer us a glimpse into the college experiences of average, in-state students at large, mid-tier public universities. Though they struggled to gain entrance to the flagship campus, they soon found that the structure of social and economic life there served them poorly—and had deleterious effects.

The nutgraf, which appears somewhere in first several paragraphs, is the main argument, or "nut" of your story. It foreshadows the rest of the argument but doesn't give everything away. It hopefully says something new. If you can defy the prevailing wisdom on the subject, all the better. In this case, Hamilton and Armstrong find that, against assumptions that college is the great leveler and the key to upward mobility, students' class distinctions often follow them throughout their university years.

But why should we believe the authors' claims? The second part of the article, after the introductory paragraphs (the hook and nutgraf), offers a very brief literature review, showing how the article is situated in some larger debates about educational achievement and class background. It places the story in a specific political context, raising questions about how universities establish their priorities, and the differential impact of these priorities on different groups of students:

> Once private universities skim off affluent, high-performing students, large, middle-tier public universities are left to compete for the tuition dollars of less studious students from wealthy families. How, we wondered, do in-state students fare in this context?

This part of the article establishes the authority of its authors and tells us why we should listen to them. We learn that they studied these students for over five years, and that they focused on one dormitory floor, conducting both ethnographic research and interviews with the young women and their parents. By this time, then, the reader knows where the article is going, why he or she should pay attention to it, and what its general argument is. We are sufficiently intrigued to keep reading, but enough mystery is built up to interest the reader in knowing more, and reading on.

The authors build their argument by showing and telling. That is, they people the story with vivid individuals who develop over time, and sometimes even come into conflict with one another. In doing so, they illuminate how processes, structures, and institutions work. A classic narrative structure focuses on an individual or small group and its quest to solve some problem or achieve some goal. Here the story focuses on these two young women and their experiences at the same university, and the challenges they face navigating through it. The larger quest is for upward mobility, perhaps even to achieve the much-vaunted American Dream, which has often been symbolized by the achievement of a college degree—even if the article complicates that narrative.

Hamilton and Armstrong take us through the different aspects of the college experience through the lives of Monica and Karen: navigating bureaucratic structures, choosing housing, dorm life, the party scene, academic struggles, and encounters with what the authors describe as "exotic majors" such as sports broadcasting. We learn that Karen, who had hoped to become a teacher, switched to this "easy major" so that she could have more time to party. Here the authors show us this process, and the dilemmas this decision raised for her, using quotes that show the respondents' distinctive voices:

> Karen explained, "I'm from a really small town and it's just all I ever really knew was jobs that were around me, and most of those are teachers." A woman on her floor was majoring in sports broadcasting, which Karen had never considered. "I would have never thought about that. And so I saw her, and I was like that's something that I really like. One of my interests is sports, watching them, playing them," she reasoned. "I could be a sportscaster on ESPN if I really wanted to."

In the following paragraph the authors tell the reader what the sociological implications of Karen's sentiments are:

> Karen's experience shows the seductive appeal of certain "easy majors." These are occupational and professional programs that are often housed in their own schools and colleges. They are associated

with a higher overall GPA and, as sociologists Richard Arum and Josipa Roksa report in *Academically Adrift*, lower levels of learning than majors in the more challenging sciences and humanities housed in colleges of arts and sciences.

In subsequent paragraphs, through techniques of both showing and telling, we learn that Karen's choice to pursue sports broadcasting was in fact a deeply problematic one. Several of Karen's wealthier peers secured plum internships. For Karen the career choice was not very practical, and she made the expensive choice of switching back to education. In the end, Monica and Karen both left MU. Nine other women from their dorm, the majority of whom were from working-class backgrounds, did so as well. Why did these flagship state universities fail so many of their students? The conclusion brings home the main point of the piece, and offers a call to action without being didactic:

> It is tempting to assume that academic success is determined, in large part, by what students bring with them—different ability levels, resources, and orientations to college life. But Monica and Karen's stories demonstrate that what students get out of college is also organizationally produced. . . . Monica and Karen's struggles at MU can be attributed, in part, to the dominance of a "party pathway" at that institution, which is designed to attract and serve affluent, socially-oriented students.

At the end of the article, the authors bring the main point home. They offer some suggestions to parents who want to figure out what schools are best for their children. They also challenge the priorities of public institutions that support easy majors and the Greek system as a way of attracting more affluent students. The best articles end with a "kicker" that refers back to the lead, telling the reader what you want them to know or do, though not necessarily explicitly.

Here we have an account of two young women, their experiences in college as they pass through the educational system, the dilemmas they encounter, and the obstacles they must overcome to attain their goals of college degrees, and, ultimately, of satisfying and secure jobs. Theirs is a journey where many of the rules are unwritten, and where the resources needed to benefit fully from the college experience are out of reach for those without considerable cultural, social, and financial capital. The article "shows," by describing the setting and its characters vividly, and it "tells" about the story of individual lives. It is a clear account of connected events that unfold through time, with characters that interact with one another. The goal is to focus on the particular to tell a bigger story about social worlds. At its best, such writing also has sensual appeal, conveying the look, sounds, and smell of a scene, as well surprise, drama, and conflict.

By offering you a basic structure of a feature article that blends journalistic and sociological techniques, we hope that you can adapt this to your own needs. (Perhaps we should have called this chapter "Unlearning Journal Article Writing"!) These guidelines should not be followed slavishly. One might find, for example, that you'd rather show than tell at times, and that rather than state your thesis early on, you'd rather bring the reader along by offering thick description. But generally, this narrative structure, which is broadly recognizable, can help you translate your work and broaden its reach. The shift to digital platforms may be heralding a return to the "long read," and more and more online magazines are cropping up that publish well-written analytic pieces on a variety of topics.

Paint a portrait of a rich, complex social life, filled with flesh-and-blood humans in shifting social worlds. Strive to be simple and direct, coherent and compelling, rather than comprehensive and complete. Use active verbs, peopling your prose rather than filling it with objects, and embody, through your writing, the belief that social change is possible. Writing clearly and engagingly can imbue our prose with ethical purpose and deepen the public conversation about things that really matter. Writing op-eds and long-form pieces can help you develop your public voice and an audience for your work, and may convince you that you have a lot more to say, perhaps even enough to fill a book—the topic of the next chapter.

... 3 ...

Books for General Audiences

In 1950, a social critic named David Riesman published a book called *The Lonely Crowd* that quickly became the topic of debate and cocktail party conversations across the land. The book made a bold thesis about the relationship between modern capitalism, American culture, and personality. It suggested that working for large corporations and living in a consumer society was changing Americans' experience of themselves and others, creating expectations that few, if any, could successfully fulfill. Capturing the zeitgeist of the fifties, *The Lonely Crowd* sold over a million and a half copies.[1] It inspired student radicals of the 1960s, and was even mentioned in a Bob Dylan song.

Books can, at times, introduce new ideas, new vocabularies, and new ways of thinking, and spark public conversations that shape the ways people understand themselves and their world. While gauging the impact of a single work is a tricky business, sales are a rough indicator of influence. Yet by one account, only fifty sociological books published in the second half of the twentieth century sold over fifty thousand copies each, and few works of "serious" social science to-day sell more than a couple thousand copies.[2] Why is this?

Some say it is because the heyday of popular sociology is over, and that psychologists and economists, along with journalists, have become the go-to experts for insightful social commentary, not sociologists. Others suggest that the problem is an even bigger one: the "educated general reader" no longer exists. Smart phones and social media, some suggest, have turned us all into instant consumers with flagging attention spans, unable to read in a sustained way. Still, some challenging, intellectually demanding books do succeed, and a handful of academics become public intellectuals by publishing well-regarded scholarly books that cross over into popular discussions.

For example, French economist Thomas Piketty's seven-hundred-page book on inequality, *Capital in the Twenty-First Century*, became a runaway hit.[3] Piketty and his countryman Pierre Bourdieu (now deceased) are unusual: they write dense tomes that engage broad audiences. Morocco's Fatima Mernissi and the United Kingdom's Stuart Hall, social scientists and social critics, also traversed scholarly and nonscholarly publics. David Graeber, an anthropologist who writes about economic issues, has gained large audiences among activists. Political scientist Corey Robin writes books and blog posts that at times generate lively debates, as do philosopher Cornel West, law professor Michelle Alexander, and economists Paul Krugman and Joseph Stiglitz, among others.

In the United States today, best-selling books about social issues tend to be written by smart journalists. Barbara Ehrenreich's *Nickel and Dimed* is essentially a participant observation study of low-wage workers trying to live on the minimum wage. In *The Tipping Point* and other books, Malcolm Gladwell mines social research to tell stories about social epidemics and how they spread, for example, in a style that appeals to a broad readership. Ta-Nehisi Coates, author of *Between the World and Me* and "The Case for Reparations," draws upon empirical social science and personal experience to write powerfully about race. And Ted Conover, in his book *Newjack* about guards at an upstate New York prison, uses ethnographic techniques, what he calls "immersive journalism."

One can imagine very boring treatments of each of these subjects. But these skilled writers capture readers' interest by introducing us to characters we can identify with, and by constructing richly detailed scenes that show these characters relating to the world around them. Ehrenreich's *Nickel and Dimed*, like the best of C. Wright Mills's works, links personal troubles and public issues, is concerned with a problem of broad social significance, and was written to be read and discussed broadly. Appealing to a general reader, it encourages them to keep reading by using wit and humor. Still, we once heard a colleague scoff: "It would never have been published in the *American Journal of Sociology*. It did not test a hypothesis." While that may be true, an article published in the esteemed *AJS* is unlikely to garner the number of readers Ehrenreich has reached, or to influence the public conversation about low-wage labor so directly.

Despite the claim that public intellectual life is dead, such examples suggest that people are still hungry for books that help us make sense of our lives. We wish to understand the impact of growing economic inequality in advanced capitalist societies, how the rise of alternative movements and cultures offer new ways of living, how changes in work and family life are transforming everyday lives, and how global flows of people and money are remaking our world. We want to understand our experiences in relation to others. The popularity of narrative nonfiction books that deal with social scientific themes suggests that people will read "serious" works if they are engaging. Yet few of us who are employed by the academy write such books.

It's partly due to the fact that our profession tends to reward specialization, not popularization. Academics publish hundreds of books about crime, media, and race each year, but contribute few broad, societal level interpretations of American life. The reward structure of scholarly life—who gets hired, tenured, promoted, and picked to receive plum grants that give us time to research and write—favors those who publish studies that are written mainly for other experts in the field. Rare is the book written by a scholar that tries to offer a "big picture" take on American society writ large, in the mode of *The Lonely Crowd*. Rarer still is the book that uses rich narrative to draw nonspecialists in and keep them reading.

Academic journals and conferences are venues for specialist works by and for experts, engaging scholars in the ongoing quest to produce knowledge. But a lot of the research we do, if framed more broadly and written more engagingly, can appeal to audiences beyond the academy. In the preceding chapters, we encouraged you to cultivate a public voice by writing shorter essays, book reviews, and commentaries. In this chapter, we introduce you to three genres of book-length social science that engage general readers, and we offer a series of general tips on writing such books, borrowing some tricks of the trade from narrative nonfiction writers.

Genres of "Popular" Social Science

The Social Trend Book

Books about social trends take an identifiable development, such as the rising number of atheists, growth in support for same-sex marriage, or increasing popularity of cohabitation before marriage, and seek to understand it better. Drawing upon interviews and survey data, they deepen our understanding about why a particular trend has emerged and what it means. For example, Arlie Hochschild's *The Second Shift* shows how women's entry into the paid labor force affects family life, leading to a double burden for employed mothers. She shows that in addition to their paid work in the labor force, women are expected to do an additional "shift," taking care of most of the household and child-care responsibilities. Interviewing fifty couples, Hochschild finds that even though women's participation in the paid labor force may give them more economic power, persistent inequalities within families create added responsibilities for wives and mothers, leading to feelings of guilt and inadequacy, as well as marital tensions.

The book takes an important topic, the tension between family and work that many, if not most, people grapple with in their daily lives, and locates its social causes, giving them a name. Rather than blame women, as conservatives are wont to do, Hochschild indicts the structure of the family, and the state, for failing to accommodate the sweeping social changes. The contemporary relevance of its subject, its prescient analysis, and its engaging writing style give the book its broad appeal.

The author introduces us to a number of families. Husbands and wives talk about how they share responsibilities of parenting and housework, but their actual lives are often less than egalitarian. She writes with authority but never talks down to readers, and she uses considerable charm and wit. For example, this excerpt from chapter 1, "A Speed-Up in the Family," pictures the pop culture image of working women, and contrasts it to the "reality" of most women's lives:

> She is not the same woman in each magazine advertisement, but she is the same idea. She has that working-mother look as she strides forward, briefcase in one hand, smiling child in the other. Literally and figuratively, she is moving ahead. Her hair, if long, tosses behind her; if short, it sweeps back at the sides, suggesting mobility and progress. There is nothing shy or passive about her. She is confident, active, "liberated." She wears a dark tailored suit, but with a silk bow or colorful frill that says, "I'm really feminine underneath." She has made it in a man's world without sacrificing her femininity. And she has done this on her own. . . . When I showed a photograph of a supermom like this to the working mothers I talked to in the course of researching this book, many responded with an outright laugh.

Note how visually arresting this vignette is, and how effectively it illustrates common—albeit highly distorted—assumptions about the "superwoman" who effortlessly balances work and family life. The vignette also offers readers a window into Hochschild's research process, creating for us a picture of an empathetic, curious sociologist who probes her interviewees, photograph in hand. The author "deftly moves back and forth between case study and generalization, in a graceful, seamless narrative," said one reviewer.[4] She shows and tells, offering a description of family life in the late twentieth century, alongside a powerful analysis of what is going on beneath the surface.

Eric Klinenberg's *Going Solo*, about the rising number of single people in American society, is another popular book that illuminates an important social trend: the rise of single living. Rather than see singles in the conventional way, as failures, as losers, as individuals who are not making informed choices, who are selfish, or who pose a threat to democratic societies, he argues quite the opposite: singledom is the product of social affluence and individual freedom. Writing for an educated reader who is interested in making sense of changing family structures and lives, Klinenberg explains complex ideas clearly, without using jargon or assuming too much specialized prior knowledge. He draws upon survey and census data as well as his own interviews to explore what is at stake in this burgeoning social trend.

The book's chapters, organized thematically, offer potential entry points for different groups of readers: young middle-class singles in the city, concerned parents, older readers who may or may not themselves be single, as well as social workers and policy makers. The introduction isn't a literature review in the typical sense. Instead of previewing the entire book, it invites the reader into the author's world, establishes his authority, and offers a tantalizing hint of what is to come if they read on. Klinenberg briefly discusses his methods, and situates the book in relation to big thinkers like Ralph Waldo Emerson, Emile Durkheim, and Walt Whitman, as well as a host of contemporary theorists, portraying them as personalities who are in debate with one another—and with whom he is in conversation. Durkheim, he tells us, is a founding father of sociology whose work on individualism tried to make sense of the sweeping changes that were occurring in the nineteenth century, and who emphasized the importance of social institutions in binding individuals to a sense of the common good.

Much as Hochschild did in *The Second Shift*, Klinenberg peoples his sociological story with individuals who are trying to create full lives despite the social constraints that surround them. Alongside big picture thinkers, we get to know ordinary individuals who were interviewed during the course of research. Because the book is organized thematically rather than chronologically, we don't really come to know individuals as they move through time, as in a journalistic account or an ethnography. Rather, we meet them in "scenes"—sections that situate people in a place—a staple of long-form narrative. These scenes offer context, providing the author with an opportunity to describe individuals and show them interacting with others. For example, Klinenberg is interested in what happened to a woman named Mary Ann, a single woman who died alone in Los Angeles, and decides to shadow an investigator for the city whose job it is to find out about individuals who die, where no one claims the body or estate.

> We start our search in the hospital's patient services office. There's a nun working there, and at first we think she might know something helpful, because when she sees Mary Ann's name on the case file, her face lights up. But it turns out she spoke to her only a few times, and she has little to offer other than the assurance that Mary Ann got good care until the end.
>
> The nun hands Emily a big plastic bag. Inside is everything Mary Ann brought with her to the hospital, and Emily starts digging through it, looking for clues. There's a fluffy blue robe. A small black purse. Prescription drugs. Baby powder. Glasses. Coupons. Typical things you would find in a woman's purse.[5]

The narrative then takes us into Mary Ann's house, turning up a few clues about who the dead woman was. This scene leads into a discussion about the challenges of living—and dying—alone. By shadowing the investigator, Klinenberg offers a sense of "being there." He also builds tension and surprise, gives us a window into the author's research process, and sets a mood. Writing about places—a hospital, a restaurant, a building, a church—he establishes settings for dramatic action. Ethnographers have easy access to scenes, but anyone can construct a scene, as Klinenberg did in the preceding passage. These and other narrative nonfiction techniques should be part of our writing toolbox.

Klinenberg doesn't come off as a pretentious academic. He does not hit readers over the head with an argument. When he wishes to signal to the reader key aspects of the work, such as the direction of the argument, or the conclusions he draws from his research, he does so subtly, without belaboring his points. He addresses his audience in a conversational style, using "we" and "you" (though rarely "I") and "consider, for example . . ." rather than using more academic kinds of signposting ("the aim of this study is to" or "this essay argues that").

Going Solo offers a survey of the pleasures and perils of single living that never devolves into uncritical celebration or finger-wagging. That doesn't mean the book is without its problems, of course. (After all, any book can be picked apart!) By focusing almost exclusively on city dwellers, Klinenberg may give us a somewhat skewed portrait of family change, overgeneralizing from the experience of affluent young singles. Some say, too, that cohabitation and single parenthood are overlapping trends that are just as important as single living. Moreover, in his effort to value single life and free it from stigma, he may underestimate the continued toll that shame takes on singletons—particularly on single women—in a couple-oriented world. None of these weaknesses can be attributed to the book's style. It is to its credit that anyone can pick it up and learn a great deal about how our society is changing.

Americans are going solo. They're also "bowling alone," according to political scientist Robert Putnam. His influential book of the same name, published in 2000, is another example of this genre of popular social science.[6] Many traditional civic, social, and fraternal organizations are dying, along with certain types of social capital, Putnam argues. Like Hochschild and Klinenberg, he alerts us to an observable social trend, goes beyond the headlines to explain why it is occurring and also what is at stake—why we should care.

The Ethnographic Study

Ethnographies paint portraits of people engaged in the business of life in particular places and times. At the same time, they also tell larger stories about social conflict, inequality, or change. Because people are drawn to stories, ethnographic books are often very appealing to broader audiences. Some of the most compelling of such studies deal with urban problems and marginality, offering glimpses into the daily lives of the poor and forgotten. Ethnographers often "study down"—that is, they research people who have less power than themselves—because they're curious, because they're social reformers at heart, and because social problems tend to be associated with those at the bottom. The department of sociology at the University of Chicago produced the first studies of hoboes, street hustlers, and prostitutes, virtually introducing urban ethnography into the academic lexicon.

Mitchell Duneier works in this tradition. *Sidewalk*, his study of street-corner booksellers in New York's Greenwich Village, looks at homelessness, poverty, and marginality in the contemporary metropolis by telling the story of one street and the street-corner booksellers who work there. In doing the research, the author worked as a vendor intermittently over the course of six years. He wrote *Sidewalk* during the Mayor Rudy Giuliani era, at a time when city government, following the conservative idea that "broken windows" breed crime, was committed to policing minor violations of municipal code, and dislocating people who make their living in the streets, such as panhandlers, unlicensed street vendors, and buskers.

In *Sidewalk*, there are colorful characters like Hakim Hasan, bookseller and "street philosopher." An educated black man who is unable to get a steady job, Hasan ends up scavenging books and selling them on the street. He reads the books, too, and is more than willing to converse with potential buyers about their virtues and deficits. Learning about the daily lives of men like Hasan, we come to see the inherent order in what appears, on first glance, as disorder. Magazine vendors employ individuals to arrive early and stake out advantageous positions, and to stand at the tables when they need to get something to eat or relieve themselves. They scavenge the city for books and magazines to sell, returning the materials to a storage locker at the end of the day. These men are not signs of a neighborhood in decay. Quite the opposite, Duneier shows us: they're just trying to be their own bosses and "earn an honest living." Far from encouraging disorder, theirs is a carefully organized, deeply moral world.

Sudhir Venkatesh describes his role as ethnographer as "as an outsider looking at life from the inside." His book *Gang Leader for a Day* portrays the lives of gang members who operate a crack ring in a Chicago public housing project. It focuses on J.T., an African American man who is one of the gang leaders, whom the author befriended early in the project and got to know intimately over the course of several years. J.T. brags to his friends that his professor friend is "writing about my life." Venkatesh shows us what J.T. does every day, how his gang is organized, how he thinks about engaging in criminal activity, and how he sees different players in his world. The author describes interactions between J.T. and his compatriots and documents his own deepening relationship with his chief informant and his development as a young "rogue sociologist." In Venkatesh's rendering, J.T. is essentially a pragmatic businessperson who is concerned with protecting and expanding his turf; the author is the somewhat naive graduate student, a foil for J.T., and, at times, a recipient of his mockery.

Gang Leader is composed of a series of richly described, connected scenes that tell the story of J.T. and his world and the author's quest to learn more about it. It draws upon exhaustive ethnographic work and presents it in a narrative style that is never didactic and reads, at times, like a good novel. When it engages with sociological literature, it does so conversationally. Here's Venkatesh talking about the academic literature on gangs:

> In most of the sociological literature I'd read about gangs—they had been part of the urban fabric in the United States since at least the late nineteenth century—the gang almost always had heated relationships with parents, shopkeepers, social workers, and the police. It was portrayed as a nuisance at best, and more typically a major menace.[7]

By integrating this discussion into the narrative, and placing it in conversation with his own research, the author deepens his analysis without breaking the narrative flow. In a scene that takes place in the housing projects where his research is situated, the author takes a stroll with J.T., surveying the building. They pass an older woman who is bent over a man who is squirming on the floor:

> "Morning, Ms. Easeley," J.T. said. The man looked like he was just waking up, but I could also smell vomit, and he seemed to be in pain. He lay right outside the incinerator room, and the garbage smelled terrible.
>
> "He's coming down," Ms. Easeley told J.T. "He said someone sold him some bad stuff."
>
> "Hmm-hmm," J.T. said disapprovingly. "They all say that when something goes bad. Always blaming it on us."

Vivid dialogue like this moves the narrative along, strengthens our understanding of the main characters and their motivations, and gives us a lot of sensory (visual and, in this case, olfactory) information about the setting. Few readers of the book have probably ever stepped foot in a public housing project, or talked with a gang leader. Venkatesh takes us into that world, and by allowing us to see it through his eyes, he demystifies it, weaving a captivating story of "outlaw capitalism," life in the so-called underclass, and the art and craft of social research.

While studying the street seems to be the preserve of male (mainly, white) researchers, some of whom seem to identify (at a somewhat safe distance) with the risk-taking swagger of their subjects, at least one celebrated—and controversial—female author, sociologist Alice Goffman, explored the lives of African Americans living in blighted urban areas by embedding herself in an economically impoverished Philadelphia neighborhood. Her book, *On the Run: Fugitive Life in an American City*, like Venkatesh's and Duneier's books, reveals the inner logic of lives that otherwise seem illogical to outsiders. Young black men are on the run, even when they haven't broken the law, she shows us. Because they are under constant surveillance by the police, they become fugitives. *On the Run* became a hit and was then picked up by a trade press, which propelled Goffman into the public eye. Its popular success was partly due to timing—it appeared during a moment of heightened consciousness about overpolicing, and during the rise of the Black Lives Matter movement. However, the book's popularity didn't insulate the author from a storm of criticism (which we discuss in chapter 6).

The best ethnographies introduce us to some memorable personalities, such as Duneier's Hakim, Venkatesh's J.T., and Goffman's Chuck: complicated people who are willing to entrust their story to someone outside of their social world, who can translate their experiences for others. Through the eyes of keen outside observers, we learn about what motivates them, how they see themselves in the world, and how they spend their days. Still, they may not be as fleshed out as they might be in a skilled journalist's or novelist's hands. In *On the Run*, for example, we learn a lot about why young black men make decisions about their lives that elude the law, but we learn little about their interests, their aspirations, or their quirks and idiosyncrasies.[8] Ethnographies tend to reduce the multiple dimensions of a person's life in order to tell a story about one or two dimensions—which tend to be driven by sociological questions.

And yet by developing character, even partially, ethnographies help us care about their subjects, and take us into unfamiliar worlds using empathy and analytical rigor. By getting into the heads and hearts of their subjects, they show us how people live and love, make a living and get by, and they offer us a deeper understanding of ourselves.

The Cultural Critique

The cultural critique book offers a sustained argument about a topic of contemporary cultural importance that goes against conventional thinking. It draws its evidence from media, popular culture, and other sources, is driven by ideas, and tends to be contrarian in tone. Americans are afraid of the wrong things. Having more choices doesn't make us happier. Growing tolerance for gays and lesbians doesn't necessarily constitute progress.

Barry Glassner's *Culture of Fear* boasts one of the longest subtitles ever: "Why Americans Are Afraid of the Wrong Things; Crime, Drugs, Minorities, Teen Moms, Killer Kids, Mutant Microbes, Plane Crashes, Road Rage, and So Much More." Mining contemporary newspaper, magazine, and television reports, it isolates, dissects, and debunks Americans' misplaced fears. It sold more than fifty thousand copies in the 1990s, aided in part by a mention in Michael Moore's documentary *Bowling for Columbine*. That Glassner is a former journalist who knows how to write in a conversational style certainly helps.

"The more things improve, the more pessimistic we become," writes Glassner. "Every few months it seems we discover a new category of people to fear: government thugs in Waco, sadistic cops on Los Angeles freeways and in Brooklyn police stations, mass murdering youths in small towns all over the country."[9] When you look at the data, he says, many (if not most) of these fears, are unfounded, or interpreted incorrectly. He provides a convincing account and critique of our culture of cascading fears.

Demented drivers are guilty of "road rage"; people have lost all sense of civility; hardened criminals stalk the streets of every small town and big city in America, waiting to pounce. Americans harbor so many misbegotten fears because some people stand to make a lot of money from fearmongering. Journalists sell newspapers and television time, so-called experts profit (such as Arnold Nerenberg, whom Glassner identifies as "America's road rage therapist," and who has been featured in dozens of television shows and magazines), and politicians get to deflect attention from other more politically sensitive areas. Glassner shows how, because of this kind of journalism, we focus on demented drivers rather than declining mass transit, killer kids rather than the easy accessibility of firearms.

The Culture of Fear spares no one. While journalists often pride themselves on being suspicious about information they are given, when it comes to a "great crime story," he writes, "a journalist will behave like the high school nerd who has been approached by the most popular girl in school for help with her science project. Grateful for the opportunity, he doesn't ask a lot of questions."[10] This culture of fear is often aligned with a right-wing agenda, one that asserts the authority of so-called experts ("gifted orators with elevated minds") and wields them against unsuspecting citizens. Today new fears crop up, often in relation to teenagers and the availability of digital communications: controversies swirl around cyber-bullying, Internet addiction, sexting, and violent video games. Some of these fears are real, but they are often overstated and unnecessarily alarming.

"Fear mongers," write Glassner, "knock the optimism out of us by stuffing us full of negative presumptions about our fellow citizens and social institutions. But the United States is a wealthy nation. We have the resources to feed, house, educate, insure, and disarm our communities if we resolve to do so."[11] The mythical hazards touted by the culture of fear, and those driven to distraction like the listeners of Orson Welles's *War of the Worlds*, can do little to solve the real problems we face. In fact, Glassner argues convincingly that fearmongering places our capacity for democratic action in jeopardy.

Another book in this genre is Suzanna Danuta Walters's *The Tolerance Trap*, subtitled "How God, Genes, and Good Intentions are Sabotaging Gay Equality" (works of popular cultural critique have a propensity for rambling subtitles, it seems). The book is a powerful rebuke to those who would say that the success of the marriage equality movement and the waning of overt antigay sentiment are proof that sexual equality and freedom have been achieved. Yes, it is true that a considerable degree of progress has been made. Young gays and lesbians do not necessarily suffer the depredations of the closet, as their elders once did; queers are more public and have more rights than ever before. But by making gay rights contingent on "we're just like you arguments," Walters asserts, the movement not only excludes those who do not conform to idealized standards, but also fails to challenge homophobic and transphobic attitudes at their core.

Walters's lively, argumentative style draws upon her readings of sociological research, activist writings, film and television shows, and her own personal history to pummel the idea that we live in a post-gay age. As she sees it, more and more Americans support same-sex marriage and believe that homosexuality is something to be tolerated. They also believe that gays and lesbians are "born that way," and should be welcomed into the family fold on that basis. This is very limited way of understanding the contributions that gays and lesbians have made to American culture, she believes. By being different from, rather than the same as the culture around them, queers bring a sense of otherness and marginality, a way of seeing, and a critical understanding of many of the institutions that surround us. If we are living in a post-gay moment, its privileges may accrue only to a select group of affluent, mostly coupled white gay men.

Each chapter is packed full of evidence culled from all manner of cultural sources: the *New York Times*, the *Onion*, Gallup Polls, political pundits, social scientists, religious broadsides, *Family Guy*, Supreme

Court rulings, and Rosie O'Donnell pronouncements. All cultural objects are viable evidence, and Walters slices and dices them at a rapid clip, playing the role of analyst, commentator, and all-around smart gal. One can hear the voice of the sassy narrator who is part sociology professor, part pundit, and part activist. We learn about Walters's experiences of visiting a sperm bank, raising a feminist daughter, growing up in the heyday of lesbian feminism, and the shame of the closet. She makes good use of metaphor ("the real lavender threat," "picket fence uniformity," "a veritable mother lode of gender stereotypes") and writes with verve, speaking to a broad audience, but never simplistically. The book can be appreciated by readers who are looking for a broad, deep, and entertaining look at the past several decades of debates about lesbian and gay life. Its breezy style makes it accessible to nonacademics—an unusual feat among those who write critically about contemporary queer issues.

These and other books offer smart, opinionated syntheses of debates wafting through the culture, wielding an array of evidence to debunk popular assumptions. They're idea-driven books written by and for people who like a good argument.

Writing for a General Audience

Books about current trends, ethnographies of different social worlds, and critiques of culture are three kinds of social scientific writing that have the capacity to cross over and attract nonacademic audiences. This is not an exhaustive list of genres of "popular" social science, to be sure, and some scholars have also tried their hand at writing memoirs, biographies, New York City guidebooks, and even self-help books.[12] There are also hybrids, such as Joshua Gamson's *Modern Families*, which melds memoir and ethnography to tell the stories of new kinds of families, or Phil Zuckerman's *Living the Secular Life*, which blends interview and survey data to describe the growing numbers of nonbelievers in the United States and what they tell us about our culture.[13] Think, too, of books like *Cannibals and Kings* by anthropologist Marvin Harris and paleontologist Stephen Jay Gould's *The Mismeasure of Man*.

While some scholars may see such books as outside the bounds of academic knowledge production, they are in fact sophisticated translations of social science for general audiences. These works of popular social science were widely reviewed, generating a host of new conversations about the nature of urban poverty, the changing roles of men and women, the politics of intelligence testing, and Americans' false fears and assumptions, among other topics. Delving outside of the world of academic publishing, even for a short time, offered their authors a chance to engage broader audiences and even, at times, satisfy their creative urges.

Books that appeal to general audiences tend to have a number of things in common: they are free of scholarly jargon, written in a language that educated readers can understand, and concerned with subjects of broad general interest. They offer readers a deeply researched, thoughtful take on something they may be curious about. And they tend to have a more conversational tone than scholarly works do. Alondra Nelson describes how she thought about two audiences as she wrote *Body and Soul*, her book about black radicalism and health care politics. Even though the book was published by a university press, Nelson "worked very hard," the sociologist says, "to walk a fine line" between "using the language that I would need to use to get tenure and to convey to people that I understood the kind of nuances of the theories and concepts that we use in our work as sociologists" and writing in ways that were "plainly stated enough that regular people who are interested in the topic" could read it without having academic expertise. "It doesn't feel untraditional at all," she says. "Because I am in part an ethnographer, and a lot of that leads to spending time with working class folks and folks of color. It just seems like an obvious thing to do."

But when Nelson chose to publish a subsequent book on genetic ancestry testing with a trade press, she was faced with the challenge of developing a more popular writing voice. Even though she avoided words like "neoliberal" and "governmentality," she says, "it was very hard to go back to paragraphs that looked perfectly fine" and rewrite them for a nonacademic audience, in keeping with the press's desires. Nonetheless, she thought that the book, and the topic, "deserved the push" that a trade press might be able to offer. "The fact that it's a trade press," she says, "signals something different to people, that it's a book that is meant to be circulated and read by more people." That the publisher, Beacon Press, dedicated a publicist to the book helps, of course. Nelson notes that even though she was very happy with the academic press that published her first book, her trade book attracted "more initial interest."[14]

No matter how engagingly they're written, not all subjects have the capacity to capture a nonacademic audience, however. Historical shifts, political crises, and popular cultural trends bring some topics to the fore, propelling some books into the public eye and knocking others off the radar. It's difficult, if not impossible, to predict what will interest the fickle "reading public." But if you believe that your research would be of interest to a general reader, we suggest that you read some best-selling works of serious nonfiction. Figure out which books you like and how their authors make them engaging. Study their techniques and try to emulate them. As a rule, we academics tend to read for content, interrogating a book's argument and evidence to evaluate whether it is a worthwhile contribution to "the literature." Instead, try to read with style in mind.

Take some time to look at how books are constructed: how the words sit on the page, how the chapters and paragraphs are organized. Listen to the author's voice and figure out whether the book renders the subject matter as effectively as it can, and if it makes you want to keep reading. Here are some further tips.

Keep the Introduction Short and Simple

Don't try to try to present the entire book in miniature at the beginning. The introduction, says editor Alane Mason, is like an "entrance hall—a place to hang up your coat, adjust to the temperature, meet your hosts, get a sense of why they have invited you over, appreciate their aesthetic sensibility and perhaps background, before stepping into the first room."[15] Rather than give away your whole argument, or even the whole "plot," use the introduction to invite the reader in, introduce the subject of the work, explain why you're writing about it—and why others should care, too.

A sure way to turn off nonacademic audiences is to begin your book with a review of the scholarly literature on your topic. You can certainly pay homage to those who came before you, acknowledging that you stand in the footsteps of giants, but be sure that you keep such discussion to a minimum, integrating it, more conversationally, into the body of the work. For example, in his book *Modern Families*, Joshua Gamson discusses debates about normalcy and deviance, and the work of literary theorist Michael Warner, in a very fluid, friendly style. He takes Warner's sometimes abstract theorizing and makes it his own, showing how it relates to the people and the families he analyzes:

> If the celebration of normalcy is politically problematic, it has some logical weirdness, too. After all, Warner points out, if by normal we mean typical, there's no great argument to be made for it; no one is really normal in the statistical sense and many of the things people seem to want—to be famous or a genius or exceptionally endowed— are statistically abnormal. And if by normal we mean nonpatho- logical, there are other ways to respond to the charge that you're a freak besides trying to be as ordinary as possible. You can measure yourself by the norms you and yours have generated and not by someone else's "yardstick of normalcy." You can refuse the stigma of pathology yet also refuse to be absorbable. You can reject the notion of pathology altogether. You can, as they say, let your freak flag fly.[16]

You can see here how the author uses existing theories and litera- ture to deepen his audience's understanding of the significance of his research. He wears his erudition as lightly as possible, and uses only as much of the literature as he absolutely needs to, leavening it with a sly turn of phrase. Follow his example, if you can. Try to punctuate different chapters with mini–lit reviews, always insuring that you are bringing readers along who may not already be familiar with such discussions, and being careful not speak over their heads.

Show People, and Societies, in Motion

The people you're writing about need to be doing something; you need to write them into "scenes," which consist of places where action unfolds. In the hallway of a Chicago housing project, we see a gang member and his lackey arguing over a botched robbery. In a high school classroom, teachers are administering a standardized test to a group of nervous students. Scenes propel the narrative along, illuminating characters' needs and wants. They introduce us to a setting, a context for the story, and allow the reader to place themselves in it.

Showing change and development over time is key. Most academic books tend to be organized thematically. But in order to make your work compelling to a nonacademic audience, you may wish to organize your chapters chronologically. Chronology, Alane Mason says, "can heighten a sense of narrative and its inherent tensions and conflicts, [and] force a degree of clarity about cause and effect (or lack thereof)."[17] Some subjects no doubt lend themselves better to this than others. Ethnographies certainly do. To the extent that you can, also try to imbue your writing with tension and surprise.

For example, when one of us (Arlene) published an ethnographic study of a bitter clash over sexual politics in small town America, *The Stranger Next Door*, she structured the book to follow one local political campaign from beginning to end, introducing us to the setting, a community in the Pacific Northwest, along with key players in the campaign—church leaders, liberal activists—and "ordinary citizens." In order to build tension and maintain her readers' interest, she waited until the end to reveal the outcome of the campaign. As social researchers, we're not writing whodunits, but we can borrow some of the elements of a good mystery novel to make our prose come alive. If you don't give it all away at the beginning of the book, people will be more interested in reading until they reach the end. Real life is filled with drama and tension, so why not make it part of our writing as well?

Make It Colorful

Scholars, especially social scientists, live for universals rather than particulars. We like to synthesize and explain rather than describe and dramatize. We tend to see ourselves as analysts, not documentarians. The fact that we must adhere to university institutional review board (IRB) requirements to protect our informants exaggerates these tendencies, and makes us even more hesitant to vividly describe people or specific locations. While journalists often use individuals' real names because they want to hold people accountable, social scientists opt to keep everyone anonymous. We tend to have a different agenda: we want to analyze the big picture, engage with scholars who came before us, and contribute to social science knowledge.

Sometimes it's very important for us downplay the individuality and hide the real identities of our informants, obscuring their distinctive look and any information that may lead readers to identify them. While we do not want to compromise our interviewees' trust, or place them in jeopardy, to the extent that we can, we should try to figure out how to describe people and settings using telling details and powerful imagery. Carefully chosen details, such as the clothing people are wearing, the look and feel of a room, or the sound of a street, can make a scene come alive for readers.[18] By describing your research setting, and taking readers along on your expedition, you can convey a feeling of "being there."

Using real names, especially if they are well-known individuals, can help readers connect with those you're writing about. Frequently, individuals will agree to use their real names if they are asked. This may or may not be appropriate, depending upon the case. Identifying someone publicly can, at times, compromise their safety. As a researcher, we must be scrupulous about how we treat our subjects and abide by IRB rules. But to the extent you can, it may be very useful for you to openly identify your respondents and write about "real" people—it can make your writing much more engaging, too.

Develop Your Voice—and Breathe

Developing your own voice, and letting some of your personality in, can also make your writing more engaging. The New Journalism of the 1970s, practiced by such writers as Tom Wolfe and Joan Didion, borrowed narrative tools that were once the domain of literature, and encouraged authors to inject their own presence in the narrative. Feminist scholars have also mined personal experience to tell stories about society, and best-selling social science authors at times infuse their books with their distinctive voices.

In some of the books discussed in this chapter, the authors themselves are characters who are present to varying degrees. In *Going Solo*, Eric Klinenberg is a measured observer, a (heterosexual) married man who is curious about the fate of those who are not. Mitchell Duneier, in *Sidewalk*, is the compassionate, somewhat geeky chronicler of urban life; and Suzanna Walters is the cheeky, fast-talking critic with attitude in *The Tolerance Trap*. Not all of us are comfortable placing ourselves in their narrative, and depending on the kind of book you're writing, it may not be appropriate to do so. Ethnographic and social trends books lend themselves fairly easily to this technique. But having a distinctive voice does not necessarily require one to write in the first person. An author's voice is simply his or her "unique authorial fingerprint," according to Theresa MacPhail, a New York University professor of science and technology studies.[19] If an author has a distinctive voice, she writes, "then we can often accurately attribute a text to its correct author even if her identity is concealed." You can tell by her habitual turn of phrase, particular way of organizing a text, or distinctive way of talking with her readers.

In graduate school, social scientists often learn how to shed their distinctive voices. Some journal editors even seem to require it. But retaining that voice can make one's prose more engaging and show that it is written by a living, breathing, human being who is passionate about a particular subject—and wishes to convey her understanding of it to others. All readers like to know something about their authors, and appreciate an author whose voice is clear and resonant, with whom they can identify.

While you're letting your authorial flag fly, let your writing breathe. Academic books tend to be dense, jam-packed with concepts, data, footnotes, and possibly tables, graphs, and charts. In popular writing, paragraphs tend to be shorter, and photographs substitute for other forms of data visualization. There may be footnotes, but not a lot of them. When writing for a general audience, be mindful of the structure of sentences, paragraphs, and chapters, and how words look on each page. Vary the length of sentences and paragraphs, and don't be afraid of using shorter sentences, and even repetition, to emphasize important points. To the extent that you can, incorporate dialogue. Instead of filling your book with block quotes, which can weigh down the narrative, keep direct quotes succinct, weaving them into the narrative wherever possible, using only the most vivid quotes and paraphrasing the rest. Remember: the structure of your prose shapes the message you convey.

Once you've written the best possible draft of a manuscript, or at least have a very good idea of what it might look like, your next job is to find someone to publish it.

Write a Book Proposal

In order to interest a press in your book, you must prepare a book proposal. The typical template for a proposal consists of five elements:

synopsis/overview; author bio; marketing; research; and chapter outline. Many presses also require one or two sample chapters. In the synopsis, which is anywhere between one and five pages, say what the book is about in the broadest way possible, and explain why you are writing it. Try to be engaging, making a strong case for why the book is important right now, and also in the longer term. Particularly if you're hoping for interest from a trade publisher, it's important to introduce readers to the story, specifying the main characters, themes, and contexts. What is the book's thesis or "takeaway"? Who is this book for?

An author bio should list your credentials for writing the book. Have you written any related books? Have you won any awards for your work, or been interviewed by national media outlets about it? In the marketing section, which will run anywhere from one to three pages, describe the target audience for the book to the best of your ability. Do you have any personal connections, such as talking heads or reporters, who could help you push the book? Academic publishers will want you to enumerate the kinds of courses that might adopt your book. Trade publishers will want you to specify what kinds of readers will be interested in your book: young adults who are preparing for college, for example, or parents and friends of LGBT people, and so forth.

The marketing section should compare and contrast your book with books on similar topics. "This is the first book to account for the rise of America's growing propensity to live more simply. While Horace Newman's *Simple Living* traces the growing revolt against consumerism, that book focuses on educated urban dwellers. My book will provide a broader overview, showing how an anti-consumerist ethos is emerging across different sectors of the American population." Try to include two to five competing titles, and how your book differs from them.

Trade presses will be particularly interested in whether you can and will actively promote the book. They will want to know how you have promoted your books in the past—via speaking tours, conference talks, and the like. If you have an extensive network of media contacts, specify whom you might approach to review and discuss your book. Commercial presses (and academic ones, increasingly) are now very interested in an author's "platform," which typically includes their social media presence. How many Twitter followers do you have? Are you on Facebook? Do you contribute to online media? If you don't have a large online presence, what other ways do you have to reach your audience? Publishers can no longer create your platform: you have to have a platform to help them sell your book. You should specify this in your proposal, if you can. Today, at a time when more and more books are published, but when publishers invest fewer resources in author tours and advertising, you are more likely to land a book contract if you already have an audience of potential readers (for more on this, see chapter 4).

In the section on research, approximately one to three pages, say what methods you've used: Did you interview people? If so, whom? Is your research based on extensive fieldwork? If so, where was it conducted? How much of the research have you completed already? How much more needs to be done?

Then, provide the book's introduction in two to five pages, and a chapter-by-chapter outline, or road map of the book. The outline should establish the structure of the book and illustrate how it will be organized. It should include pithy chapter titles. Instead of "The Effects of Dyadic Withdrawal on Cohabiting Couples," write something more along the lines of "The Pleasures and Pressures of Living Together." Write anywhere from a paragraph to a page or two about what you will accomplish in each chapter, listing them in order. Finally, the sample chapter (or chapters) is very important in demonstrating to editors how you write the book. They will be looking at content, style, format, and voice. Use subheadings to organize the material, if you wish. Be sure that the material in the chapter corresponds to what you've promised in the chapter outline.

Once you've prepared the strongest possible proposal, you should query editors about whether they'd like to take a look at it. Find out who the social science acquisition editor is at a press that you're particularly interested in publishing with, and send them a friendly e-mail piquing their interest in your manuscript and asking whether they might be interested in seeing the proposal. If you're an as-yet-unpublished author, chances are they'll want to see the full manuscript before they offer you a contract. If you have contacts with individuals who have worked with the editor previously, that helps a lot.

The process of publishing with trade, or commercial presses, is often less direct. They don't exactly have an open-door policy for aspiring authors; there are entire guidebooks devoted to the question of "how to get a contract with a commercial press." Trade presses often negotiate through a go-between: a literary agent. If you think your book is particularly timely, or earth-shattering, and that it might be of interest to a commercial publisher, you should consider making contact with an agent and try to interest them in your project. The best place to find an agent is through personal connections. Or do an Internet search for agents that have represented books you admire, and approach one or more of them. In the end, the press you publish with influences, but does not determine, who gains access to your work.

Find a Publisher

What type of publisher should you seek out? There are excellent university presses (such as Princeton University, the University of California, New York University, Rutgers University, and the University of Chicago, among others), for-profit scholarly publishers (Routledge, Palgrave Macmillan, and others), commercial trade presses (such as Farrar, Strauss & Giroux, Knopf, Penguin, Norton, and the like), and nonprofit, niche publishers (such as Beacon or The New Press). There is a bit of overlap among them; for example, some large academic presses, such as Oxford, have trade divisions.

Generally speaking, commercial publishers publish books they believe can appeal to broad public audiences rather than specialists in a particular field. They tend to have more marketing and distribution muscle, and can push books more strongly when they wish to, and they dominate the mainstream review media. That's not necessarily because such books are better or more important, but simply because commercial publishers have more resources with which to advertise, market, and promote their books and authors.

As a rule, large commercial presses can also afford to pay authors larger royalty advances, though there is considerable variation in such payouts, and publishing with a trade press is no guarantee of a large advance. Because they want their books to make money, or at least earn back the advances they give authors, trade presses may be more likely to place prominent ads, arrange appearances on radio or television, or even send authors on a book tour, though these are becoming less and less common. But trade presses tend to favor stars, and less-than-stellar authors may be more apt to get lost in the shuffle.

While publishing with a trade press can propel your book into the public eye, many trade books quickly end up in the remainder bin. If a particular book fails to sell well during the first weeks, or months, after publication, or fails to garner good reviews, a trade publisher may quickly cut its losses and put its promotional effort elsewhere. Conversely, while many university and nonprofit presses simply don't have the resources needed to do mass marketing and distribution, some do, and university press books can, at times, break out and garner attention if they're particularly timely, controversial, or engaging. (For example, the University of Chicago Press recently published a book about beards that became a surprise crossover hit, getting attention in many major media outlets.) While producing books by scholars for scholars and their students is mainly what they're dedicated to, when a book has crossover potential, university presses—in part because they tend to be smaller than the trade presses, and less commercially driven—can lavish a great deal of attention on particular books. The same is true of some small niche presses.

Historically, trade publishers have been more likely to market and distribute a book beyond academic audiences, but less likely to keep that book in print—termed the "backlist"—if it doesn't keep selling well. In this age of on-demand print and e-book publishing, that is changing. If you see your core audience as students and academic readers, you may want to have the rights to your work revert back to you after a certain period of time, so that you can share a copy of it online. (We discuss this in further detail later). No matter what type of press you choose to publish with, having an editor who "gets" your book and believes in you as an author, who is willing to advocate on your behalf and make your work even better, is key.

Revise and Rewrite, and Revise Again

For all but the very best writers, what you eventually see on the page is the product of multiple drafts and a great deal of back-and-forth with an editor. "Good books aren't written, they're rewritten," says Ilene Kalish of New York University Press. In order for a great book to get written, "revision, rewriting, and editing must happen."[20] If some popular authors make writing look easy, it's because, Sudhir Venkatesh suggests, "they have an army of editors who help them to craft ideas." The editor's job is to help translate academic prose into writing that is lively and engaging. Editors can help academic authors channel a typical reader, clarify ideas that are obscure, turn limpid prose into lively prose, and insure continuity and coherence. If your editor doesn't understand your writing, Venkatesh reminds us, "you haven't figured out your message."[21]

All presses copyedit book manuscripts once they're accepted for publication, but relatively few do major conceptual editing: smoothing out the prose, clarifying arguments, and so forth. That may be particularly true of university presses. That's why individuals who decide to publish with university presses sometimes employ freelance editors to "doctor" their books and help prepare them for publication. Academics who choose to publish with commercial presses describe the painstaking, often ruthless process of working with in-house editors who may go through manuscripts with a fine-tooth comb. Making scholarly work fit for mass consumption can, at times, lead trade press editors to demand revisions that oversimplify and flatten the complexity of an argument. Working with editors can be a difficult balancing act: authors try to protect the integrity of their ideas while editors try to make them more accessible. But most people we know who have worked with talented editors suggest that they have learned a great deal from the process, and some even come to see their work as collaborative.

Conclusion

Today, publishers are on the lookout for writing that is engaging, that documents interesting research, and that translates it for others. There are some wonderful tellers of sociological stories, people who traverse the boundaries of journalism and the social sciences, showing us social phenomena and telling us what they mean. Readers pick these books up because they are interested in their subject matter, and they read them because the stories they tell about real people are entertaining and enlightening.

In their quest to sell books, popularizers do at times dumb down ideas. They don't have to be as concerned with the integrity of their evidence as a professional social scientist would be. They're not engaged in debates with a universe of scholars, and are not accountable to them. But popular sociology need not be "less than," or superficial. It takes a skilled writer and clear thinker to write for a broad public. If we focus exclusively on producing scholarship that is ever more methodologically rigorous, we cede the public sphere to journalists, celebrities, and reality-television stars. Rather than deride "popular" social science, let's reclaim it. By making great writing a central part of our craft, we can learn to produce work that is as compelling and interesting as the subjects we study.

... 4 ...

The Digital Turn

"Public engagement is very much a two-way process, and digital media really enables that," says UK-based researcher Charlotte Mathieson. For her, public engagement is about communicating research with wider audiences, and about finding ways to get those audiences to connect with what's relevant and interesting in her research. For Mathieson, "digital media has been fundamental." When she started blogging, "it was always about connecting up my research [on Victorian literature] with contemporary narratives, or finding ways in which my research could shed different perspectives on those narratives," she says. Blogging gave her a way to experiment with narratives, while Twitter gave her a platform "to find an audience with which to engage." For Mathieson, it's not only about sharing fully formed ideas. "Digital media has also helped me to shape ideas, through conversations about my online writing—public engagement is very much a two-way process, and digital media really enables that."[1]

Like Mathieson, many scholars find that digital media has enabled them to enrich their thinking and expand their professional networks, making them more international and democratic. One survey of academics who use digital media shows that it enables them to expand their professional networks, often in unpredictable, serendipitous ways.[2] Junior scholars and graduate students find that they can more easily interact with senior academics. A number of graduate students and early career researchers report that social media connections provide both emotional and intellectual support, which they find particularly important at that stage of their academic career.[3]

Digital technologies enable us to connect people and ideas across geographic distances and time zones. They make much of the information that was once only available in hard copy in brick-and-mortar libraries accessible anywhere. They have led to a shift from static websites to user-generated content, and the growth of social media—sometimes called Web 2.0.[4] How is the digital turn changing the way we do our jobs as scholars? What are some of the new tools at our disposal? How can we use them to engage in public scholarship that makes a difference? We explore these questions in this chapter.

The Rise of Digital Technologies

During the past twenty years, digital technologies have rapidly expanded, in terms of the types of devices and their functions; at the same time, they have diminished in size and cost. Computers that once filled entire buildings or rooms can now easily fit into the least expensive smart phone. For those of us who were adults before the digital turn, once familiar analog ways of doing things are being supplanted by the digital. For those born after about 1993, the digital is simply the way things are. Whichever group you fall into (or somewhere in between), digital technologies are changing the ways scholars communicate and do their jobs.

When we need to locate a reference, we no longer comb through a card catalog in a library. Instead, we use an online database through our library's website, or look up citations using Google Scholar. Libraries are increasingly digital and distributed. For example, the Digital Public Library of America began as an entirely digital endeavor, rather than a brick-and-mortar building. Digital technologies are also changing how we keep track of the citations we find. With tools like Zotero, we can collaboratively create and share bibliographies and share them with other scholars who have similar interests. Digital technologies are also changing how scholars write peer reviews and communicate with one another. Platforms such as Wordpress enable just about anyone to start their own blog, share first drafts of scholarly papers, and, using blogging tools such as the commenting feature, make peer review a more open, transparent process.

The web, as we know it today, was invented as a way for researchers to communicate with one another. It took a while for this remarkable, open, and free innovation (by Tim Berners-Lee in 1990) to dramatically transform scholarly communication. In the early days, academics sometimes used the Internet to share academic papers through e-mail. A few of us hand-coded personal webpages in HTML. In the decade that followed, the Internet became ubiquitous in workplaces and households throughout the United States and much of the global North.

By 2005, the technology required to easily update a webpage without knowing any HTML coding became widespread and the neologism "blog"—short for weblog—was declared the "word of the year" by Merriam-Webster. Academics were enthusiastic bloggers, and many scholars demonstrated a talent for writing for a broad audience. Blogs not only offer users an easy way to update a page; they also allow readers to comment and react to posts. While this may seem obvious now, websites were once just things you looked at, and you couldn't interact with them.

With the rise of blogging, social media platforms began to alter the web, and make their way into the academy. Since it launched in 2006, Twitter has figured prominently in this change.[5] Academics across a range of disciplines are adopting Twitter—as of 2011, roughly one in forty scholars—and its continued growth is fairly certain.[6] It is being used in the classroom by scholars who wish to manage their professional identities (more about this later on). It is also a place to make connections and conduct research, and a way to create a network of scholarly influence.[7]

As we've moved from analog ways of dealing with information to binary code (0's and 1's), information has become easier to move around, edit, and analyze. Think for a moment about what the term "cut and paste" originally meant. This term was once used to describe the process of physically cutting printed text on paper using scissors, and then pasting the text in different order using glue or tape. Now, when we use the term we're usually referring to the ways that simple keystrokes allow us to rearrange text on a screen. The move from printed-text-and-glue-based analog "cut and paste" to the keystroke "cut and paste" suggests how easy it has become to manipulate data in digital form.

Legacy Models of Academia

"Legacy scholarship," as we use the term here, refers to a set of analog practices that are common throughout academic professions. In the legacy model, the only options for publication were printed and bound volumes that were held in brick-and-mortar libraries, which circulated exclusively among people in similar institutions. The assumption underlying this model of academic life was that scholars were producing knowledge for a closed circle of specialists in their own field. This kind of publishing is concerned mainly with peer review inside the academy, and is far less engaged in communication with the broader world. In sum, the legacy model of scholarship derives from twentieth-century (and earlier) practices of print-only publication, in volumes intended for small groups of specialized readers, focusing inward, on the scholarly world.

Legacy models of academia are rooted in modes of knowledge production fashioned in an analog-dominant epoch. Yet old traditions live on even after they're outmoded. Take the case of the robes and tams that academics don for graduation and matriculation ceremonies. Some of the very earliest scholars toiled in the chilly halls of unheated buildings at Oxford and Cambridge Universities, and thus wore long robes to keep warm. Eventually, the robes came to designate high academic status and were embellished with variously colored hoods and tams, indicating wearers' affiliation with specific institutions. Today, of course, it would seem preposterous if someone suggested we wear robes all of the time. Yet the fact that we still wear robes at all indicates how academia can, at times, venerate outmoded practices. Robes and tams may be fun for graduation ceremonies, but they're no longer practical for everyday wear.

Many of our methods of teaching are also rooted in legacy systems and twentieth-century models of industrial production, according to historian of technology and educational theorist Cathy N. Davidson. She contends that the practice of lining up and bolting students' seats to the ground, in regimented columns and rows, with a teacher at the helm, was designed to instill the kind of work habits that conformed to conditions of industrial capitalism. In the twenty-first century, a generation of students who have grown up with digital technologies, are entering a very different kind of workforce. These students, Davidson argues, require a very different kind of learning than the twentieth-century version currently on offer.[8]

Digital scholarship, like legacy scholarship, is a set of practices rather than a single field of study. It is rooted in modes of knowledge production, distribution, and pedagogy that utilize computer and Internet technologies—not only to replicate activities that were possible using analog technologies, but also to develop new academic practices, including new ways of engaging in public scholarship. Within the paradigm of digital scholarship, there are a range of options for publication that include printed and bound volumes available in brick-and-mortar libraries, and e-versions of those publications available through library databases.[9]

Digital scholarship is simultaneously concerned with both rigorous peer review by highly trained specialists and open-access publishing platforms that can enable authors to reach a general audience. Underlying this model of academic life is an ethos of openness in relation to the production of and dissemination of knowledge. "Digital scholarship," as we define this term, encompasses the disciplines included in the digital humanities (literature, history, rhetoric, and composition), Internet studies, and digital sociology. The digital model of scholarship is rooted in twenty-first-century practices of online publication, open-access distribution, and rigorous peer review—sometimes open peer review or postpublication peer review. It is also steeped in a foundational concern with the world beyond the academy.

This shift from analog to digital has been incomplete and uneven. At many institutions, advisors and more senior colleagues discourage graduate students and early career scholars from engaging in any form of digital scholarship until "after tenure." At the other extreme, entire departments and new hires are foregrounding digital scholarship. In the vast, messy middle are the majority of institutions, departments, and schools, where graduate students, early career scholars, and sometimes more senior scholars pursue digital scholarship and must educate their advisors, deans, and tenure committees about the value of such work. (Chapter 7 discusses how to demonstrate the impact of digital scholarship for such audiences.)

Scholarship after the Digital Turn

The digital turn is transforming everyday practices of creating and accumulating knowledge. Writing practices are changing. Note taking, often the start of the research process, has become digitized, along with systems for filing notes. Computerized word processing enables quick and easy editing. And now that journals are fully online, to access articles we no longer need to locate printed copies on library shelves and then photocopy the desired pages. Scholars are developing a set of habits for using search engines, making decisions about what information is important and what is not.[10]

The digital turn is changing peer review, making it more open, transparent, and useful. This is perhaps most evident in the humanities, where digital models of scholarship have been evolving for more than twenty years. Some humanities scholars have used this digital technology to compile entire books that have subsequently been published by well-regarded academic presses. For example, Kathleen Fitzpatrick used Wordpress and Commentpress to develop her book *Planned Obsolescence*, which ponders the potential of digital technology to reconnect humanities scholars with broader social debates, policy makers, and general readers.

Before seeking out a publisher for the book, Fitzpatrick spent several years writing about these ideas on her blog, and then shaped those early blog posts into the Commentpress platform, opening it up to peer reviewers. The people who commented on her work in progress were not anonymous; they ranged from the high-level experts in her field one would typically expect to review her work, to graduate students at other institutions, to interested intellectuals and nonspecialists from around the world. After a period in the open peer-review phase, Fitzpatrick published the book with a university press. (Readers can still see Fitzpatrick's earlier blog posts with her ideas in formation on the Commentpress site. For its part, New York University Press makes one chapter of the book available for free through its website.[11])

Today, people can read and share Fitzpatrick's work in many ways. A wide audience of academics and nonacademics can access and discuss her work, which was subject to rigorous (but not anonymous) peer review. Reflecting on this experience, Fitzpatrick writes that these new platforms are changing the way we think about publication, reading, and peer review: "Distinction is no longer associated with publication, but instead with reception, with the response produced by a community of readers."[12] She contends that these technologies are broadening the definition of peer review to include specialists inside the academy, as well as those outside.

Fitzpatrick argues that the current system of peer review is deeply flawed, even broken. She contends that the closed communication between reviewer and editor excludes authors and impedes the circulation of ideas. Fitzpatrick says that our supposedly "blind" peer-review system is an outdated measure of authority that is at risk of becoming irrelevant—or obsolete—in an online environment where the identity of authors, and reviewers is easily discoverable. Instead, she suggests that we begin to adopt open peer review, where the authors and reviewers are openly identified. This way more voices and ideas circulate, and the review process becomes more of a conversation and less of a hazing ritual. However, Fitzpatrick acknowledges that for open peer review to work, it will require mechanisms for offering credit for serving as a peer reviewer.[13]

There are many models of open peer review—signed review, disclosed review, editor-mediated review, transparent review, crowd-sourced review, prepublication review, synchronous review, and post-publication review—across a wide range of scholarly disciplines.[14] The point is that the digital turn means that the legacy model of being an academic is undergoing a profound change.[15] At the same time, new tools are emerging for the digital scholar.

Some Tools for Digital Scholars

From blogging to Twitter, academics are increasingly dialoguing with wider publics that include elected officials, journalists, and ordinary citizens. Digital media technologies can be part of the larger model of digital scholarship, rather than simply a tool for disseminating to the "outside" world research that's created "inside" the academy.

In a survey of academics' social media practices, sociologist Deborah Lupton found that the most popular sites were (in order of popularity) Twitter, LinkedIn, Academia.edu, Facebook, Research-Gate, a personal blog, YouTube, and online referencing tools, such

Text Box 4.1 From Tweet to Journal Article

Digital media is changing how I (Jessie) do my work as a scholar. How I work today bears little resemblance to the way I was trained as a scholar, but has everything to do with being competent with both scholarship and digital technologies. To illustrate what I mean by this, let's look at the story behind a recent article of mine that started with a tweet at an academic conference, then became a blog post, then a series of blog posts, and eventually an article in a peer-reviewed journal.

The germ of an idea that became my article "Race and Racism in Internet Studies: A Review and Critique" began at the American Sociology Association Annual Meeting in 2010.[1] I attended sessions about online discourse and, given my interest in racism, I kept expecting someone to bring up this issue.

I was disappointed by the lack of attention to racism, or race more generally, in the sessions I attended, and tweeted that observation, using the hashtag of the conference (#asa2010). When I consulted the program for the conference I was truly perplexed to find that the only session on race and digital media was the one I helped organize. In a lot of ways, a tweet is just a "sound bite" in 140-characters of text. And, as the astrophysicist Neil deGrasse Tyson suggests, there's nothing wrong with a sound bite, especially if you want to reach a wider audience than just other specialists in your field.

That one tweet—and the dearth of scholarship it spoke to—got me thinking about the kinds of sessions I would like to see at the ASA, and the sorts of things I thought sociologists should be studying, so I wrote a blog post about it: "Race, Racism & the Internet: 10 Things Sociologists Should Be Studying." As I usually do now, I shared that blog post via Twitter.

Many people shared their work with me, along with the work of their students, friends, and colleagues—in the form of comments to the blog or @replies on Twitter. Suggestions for further citations came from people I know almost exclusively through our interactions via the blog or Twitter. That feedback—from geographically remote and institutionally varied, yet digitally close, colleagues—got me thinking about expanding that single blog post into a series of posts. I wanted to review the wide range of interdisciplinary work happening in what Ess and Dutton call "Internet studies." Why bother with this, one might reasonably ask?

Central to my new scholarly workflow is the blog *Racism Review*, which I started in 2007 with sociologist Joe Feagin to create an online resource for reliable, scholarly information for journalists, students, and members of the general public who are seeking solid evidence-based research on and analysis of "race" and racism. The blog is, for me,

1. Charles Ess and William Dutton, eds., special issue, "The Rise of Internet Studies," *New Media & Society* 15, no. 5 (August 2015): 695–719.

(*continued*)

a central part of my scholarship. I use it to post first drafts of ideas, keep up-to-date on the research literature, and since I firmly believe that writing is thinking, to work out just what I think about something.

The blog has also become a way to support other scholars both in their research and in teaching. A number of academics have told us that they use the blog in teaching. Kimberley Ducey, a Canadian scholar, uses *Racism Review* blog posts in an instructor's manual for a traditional introductory sociology textbook as lecture suggestions, in-class activities, and essays/assignments. Through the many guest bloggers we host, I learn about other people's scholarly work that I might not otherwise know about. The blog has become a mentoring platform, where early career scholars often get started with blogging and then go on to create their own. Since it is content-hungry, I'm always thinking about scholarship that might make an interesting blog post.

From late February to early March 2011, I created a series of blog posts that expanded on the initial "10 Things" post from August 2010. Those posts were all about the current scholarship on race, racism, and the Internet, with each one focusing on a different subfield in sociology, including Internet infrastructure and labor force issues; digital divides and mobile technology; racist social movement groups; social networking sites; dating; housing; and the comments sections of news and sports sites. This last area, racism in comments sections, prompted a research collaboration with one of the presenters from that 2010 ASA session I organized, and our paper was eventually published in the journal *Media, Culture & Society*.

At about the same, I spotted a call for papers for a special issue on Internet studies at fifteen years into the field. So I combined all of the blog posts into one paper, and thought more about what my critique of the field as a whole might be. I ended up revisiting some of Stuart Hall's earlier writing about the "spectacle" of race in media scholarship, discussing that in relation to Joe Feagin and Sean Elias's critique of "racial formation" as a weak theoretical frame for Internet studies. The paper went into an extended peer review process, I revised it once, and it finally appeared online, ahead of print, in December 2012, and in print in August 2013.

Except for the very end of this process—submitting the paper to the journal for peer review—none of this way of working bears the least bit of resemblance to how I was trained to be a scholar. My primary job as an academic is to create new knowledge, traditionally measured by the number of articles and books I produce. Traditional graduate school training has taught us to think of a "pipeline" of notes, posters, conference papers, journal submissions (and/or book proposals), revisions, resubmissions, and, finally, print publication. For me, being a scholar now is completely different than when I went to graduate school because of the ways digital media infuses pretty much every step of the research and publication process.

The story I've described here—from a tweet at an academic conference, to a blog post, to a series of blog posts, to a paper that became an article—is just one of many possible iterations of how to be a scholar today using digital media.

Other permutations might include live-tweeting an article you're reading. Sometimes, for example, when I get preset "alerts" in my e-mail about newly published scholarship I'm interested in, I will share a title and a link via Twitter. If, upon reading further, I find the piece especially perspicacious, I may share select sentences via Twitter. If it happens that there's a current event in the news that the article can help illuminate, then I'll draft a blog post that incorporates it.

From where I sit, being a scholar now involves creating knowledge in ways that are more open, more fluid, and more easily accessed by wider audiences.

---

as Zotero.[16] Other sites like Tumblr, Slideshare, and Google Scholar came in way behind. In what follows, we offer some guidance about the best practices for using some of these tools for engaging wider audiences through social media. But a caveat before we proceed: Most digital media technologies are commercially owned and operated. That means, among other things, that companies and their services can and do go away. They merge with some other company, get bought out, sell out, or just plain cease to exist. In the following, we describe the current range of technologies public scholars are using, along with recommendations about how to use them for your purposes—though some of these will surely have changed by the time you are reading this.

Your Name, Your Domain

The default web presence most (full-time) academics have is a faculty webpage set up by someone at their institution. These institutional web affiliations, like institutional e-mail addresses, can be useful for establishing legitimacy and are sometimes necessary for conducting the business of being an academic (such as ordering desk copies of text books), but they are inadequate for the needs of the contemporary public scholar. Public scholars working today, whether full-time or part-time, need a web presence that they can control.

Digital strategist and academic Jim Groom emphasizes the importance of "owning one's own domain." He even requires his students to register their own name as a domain (for example, ShawntaSmith .com or ShawntaSmith.org.) in their first year of college. Groom teaches students how to use the domain as a portfolio for their work as undergraduates. Sadly, those in graduate school rarely receive such training; nor do new faculty members.

For scholars who want to engage with wider audiences beyond a few specialists in their fields, owning your own domain name is a good first step. You can then link your other social media accounts and profiles to this domain. The easiest place to start is go to one of the many domain registrars—there are hundreds, perhaps thousands of these, so ask around (eNom is a good one; avoid GoDaddy if you can). Once you're there, type in the first and last name that you use professionally to see if it's available as a domain name. If it is, stake your claim on that little corner of the web with a few of your hard-earned dollars (around $10 or $15). This is a great beginning, and you can hold on to that domain name as long as you renew it promptly according to the registrar's terms. Be wary of "cybersquatters" who will buy up your domain quickly if you don't renew it with your domain registrar.

Getting your domain name pointed to a website involves a few more steps. What you need next is a web host. This is different than the registrar. The web host actually hosts, or stores, your website on one of their computers and makes it easy for the world to find your corner of the web. As with registrars, there are hundreds of web-hosting companies. Ask a friend who they use and what their experience has been like, or check online to see how the web host is rated. The prices are fairly consistent, but there's a lot of variation in customer service and how responsive they are. You'll want to find one that you can reach easily and that will respond quickly if you have an issue (like your site is down for no reason you can figure out).

Once you select a web host, you'll need to get the domain to point to the website. What this entails will vary depending on what kind of site you're setting up, and it is probably the most technically challenging part of setting up your own site. Sites like Jimdo, Squarespace, Weebly, and Wix (you can find them by adding ".com" to these names on the web) are intended for people with no web-design skills to be able to build a website. Most of them use a "what you see is what you get" interface that makes them pretty easy to use, even for the novice. If you want to learn even more about how to build your own site, we recommend that you go to Lynda.com, which has lots of great video tutorials about web development.

Blogs

Maintaining a blog is typically a long-term proposition—and a lot of work. That said, you can start blogging without creating your own blog. Many academic blogs are group blogs with multiple authors. (Check out *Savage Minds*, *Somatosphere*, *Social (In)Queery*, or *Cybergology*, for a start.) Scholarly blogs frequently look for new contributors. Check the blog for submission guidelines, which are often posted, or send an e-mail to the blog managers describing what you want to write and see what they say. It's usually a good idea to include some sort of institutional affiliation, a little about your educational background, and what your idea for a blog post involves. Ask them what format they would like it in (Word.doc, plain text in an e-mail, or if they want to send you log-in credentials and have you write in the blog platform itself). And be sure to see if they have a particular editorial schedule (we only do stories about puppies on Mondays; unicorn stories only appear on Fridays). Academic blogs typically do not pay for submissions from guest bloggers.

If you decide that you want to start your own blog, there are lots of tools available to do so. The most popular platform right now is Wordpress, which has two versions. Wordpress.com is the "hosted" version, meaning that Wordpress hosts the site for you. It's intended for beginners, so it's easy to set up a blog and get going right away. That said, it's more difficult to customize it once you've started. And because it is a commercial enterprise, once you have a blog there, the interface will try to sell you things—upgrades, new features. If these ads annoy you, the adventure will prove to be frustrating. Wordpress .org is the "self-hosted" version, which means you'll have to find a web host for your blog. While this takes a little more skill to set up initially, it will give you a lot more flexibility about configuring it (again, with some skills). It's also advertisement free, so that's a plus.

Blogging software allows for comments on each post and sometimes these can be engaging places of spirited conversation about intellectual ideas, sort of an online version of a small academic conference session. Once you've selected the platform you're going to use for your blog, there are many ways to get started. You can blog about your own research findings or process, and then share that blog post through Twitter. People may respond to you on Twitter rather than in the comments section your blog, and that's fine. Just keep in mind that the kinds of conversations you can have in the 140-character format may be different from those that happen in the comparatively unfettered comments section on a blog post. Instead of writing about your own research, you could use your scholarly blog to highlight the work that others are doing in your field.

For example, Jessie frequently writes a "Research Brief" post that includes some of the latest academic research related to race and racism. She gleans these new research titles through a set of Google Scholar alerts that automatically generates e-mails with links to recent publications around keywords that she's selected. Another strategy for your scholarly blog is to write a reaction to a news event that is related to your area of research. Or you can create your own mix of all these kinds of entries at your blog. Your blog could provide a hub for ideas or approaches that get little attention. Perhaps you're interested in the history of photographs and medicine, the place where popular culture and criminal justice overlap, or whatever your set of interests might be. By establishing a scholarly blog, you create a distinctive place online where other people who share your interests can find information about that particular area.

Keep in mind that an individual blog post typically contains three elements: (1) well-written prose; (2) hyperlinks to other sites; and (3) at least one image or video.

What constitutes well-written prose on a blog is not going to sound the same as a journal article. When thinking about how to develop your voice online as a public scholar, it's useful to think of a bright, nonspecialist friend or colleague as the ideal audience. Whatever the "imagined community" of readers, keep the prose smart, lively, and engaging for a broad, general audience.

Finding your voice online can be challenging, but the key is to be smart and engaging. You don't want to dumb down your work if you're blogging, but you do want to keep in mind that you're trying to reach an audience of nonspecialists in your field. In thinking about "voice" on scholarly blogs, some people find it useful to imagine an audience of very smart, sympathetic but beginner-level students who are eager to hear your explanation of some current event. Lester Andrist learned this at the *Sociological Cinema* when they shared a political cartoon that was related to a current event. People loved the post, and by the end of the day more people had liked the page than during the entire previous month. By posting the cartoon on their site, they were implicitly approving of the cartoon's political position, and people seemed to respond positively. "I think it was one of the first moments that *The Sociological Cinema* had a voice or an identity, as opposed to simply being a warehouse of teaching resources." That voice, Andrist says, developed into a distinct identity as three politically conscious, public sociologists who share an interest in visual pedagogy.

Social media is really about networks, and the digital era makes networks more salient than ever. Hyperlinks in blog posts are important because they are pathways of connection. Hyperlinks to another blog from yours create "pingbacks," or notification trails, from your blog to the blog you linked to in your post. Each time you include a hyperlink in your blog, the link goes out and sends a "ping" back to the blog's owner. These are one of the main ways that scholars who are blogging find each other's work online. When they're done well, scholarly blogs can help you build an audience for your research (more about that in chapter 5).

Even if you don't create a scholarly blog that features images, like *Sociological Images*, people expect to find images and videos in your posts, so be sure to include an image (or video) in each post. When you do, try to avoid using copyrighted images or media that you don't have permission to use. Or create your own images. There are lots of tools available, like Piktochart (www.piktochart.com) or MemeGenerator (www.memegenerator.com), which are currently free and allow you to easily create compelling images that you could post on your blog. While these specific tools may not last, there will likely be others that emerge to help you create images that people will want to share.

In creating images for your blog, Creative Commons licensing comes in handy. Creative Commons is an alternative to copyright that encourages sharing, reuse, and remix of content. What you really want to happen is for people to see the image, share it, and link back to you, or at least give you credit for creating it. You may even want people to create their own version of the image and text. If you designate the image, or even your entire blog, with a version of a Creative Commons license, that ensures people will give you credit ("attribution") and that they won't use it for profit ("non-commercial"). If you also indicate that the image is "share-alike," then you're indicating that other people need to share the images they've created and posted online in the same way you've shared your content. Because this alternative to copyright allows for remix and reuse, it makes possible new ways of building an audience online, like memes.

Say you create an image with some text and post it to your blog, as Danielle Henderson did when she started *Feminist Ryan Gosling*. Henderson remixed an existing meme—a meme is just a funny image, video, or bit of text that's copied with slight variations and spread rapidly through the Internet—and she made it her own. Henderson, who was a graduate student in gender studies at the time, says that she wanted to "keep track of theorists I was studying" and thought it might help to create "feminist flash cards." Since there's the Internet, of course, she did this online.

Over each image of the celebrity she posted, Henderson added text with quotes of feminist theory or quips about gender inequality, each one beginning with "Hey girl." One of them, for instance, features a sultry Gosling in a plaid flannel shirt, arms folded across his chest, looking directly into the camera, and the caption reads: "Hey girl. My perfect Saturday is a hot cup of tea at sunrise, a trip to the farmer's market, and curling up on the couch to figure out bell hooks' theory that feminism is a struggle to eradicate the ideology of domination that permeates Western culture with you."[17] Henderson certainly found an audience—partly through an image and accompanying text that could be remixed and shared again. She also touched on one of the key elements of Internet culture: humor. Things that are funny are shared more widely. And, for a particular audience, *Feminist Ryan Gosling* was incredibly funny. The meme spread quickly and proved to be very popular, with 3 million viewers of the site per month and some thirty thousand followers of the Tumblr she created. As a result of her success at finding an audience she didn't know existed, Henderson got a literary agent and released a trade press book.[18]

While some say that blogging is dying out, the reality is that blogging technology is just "baked into" other platforms and technologies. Although some platforms like Google's Blogger do in fact appear to be heading toward obsolescence (no support or new features for several years), there are more than a dozen blogging and publishing platforms that are new, very much alive, and attracting new users.[19] Wordpress is at the top of the list, along with Squarespace, which we mentioned a bit earlier in the section on building your website. That's what we mean by "baked in"—with the same tool (Squarespace) you can build a static website that you can use as a portfolio showcasing your work, and you can add a blog to that site for interactive publishing. There are a few other tools you might find useful.

Twitter

Academics who are skilled at writing long, nuanced, complex arguments may be flummoxed by the 140-character constraints of Twitter. But they needn't be. Twitter can be a great way to find your tribe, the particular set of people who share your research interests, or even your sense of humor.

Sure, there's a Twitter lingo, but it's not that hard to learn. The first term you should know is the "handle," or the name you use on Twitter. When you choose a handle, you want it to be something that's short (your handle takes up part of your allotted 140 characters). And you want something that's easy to remember. Take a few minutes to set up your profile with a bio that describes a little about your interests, and upload a recent photo. Figure out what you want to contribute to the conversation on Twitter. For academics, think about sharing the latest news in your field. Did a recent journal article you read seem especially pathbreaking for people in your field? Compose a tweet about that, and then people will begin to look to you for the latest news in that field. Next, find people you want to connect with. Re-tweet them. Talk to them. Connect with them.

One of the most useful implementations of Twitter is at academic conferences. For the uninitiated, the junior, the marginalized, or the just-plain-shy, academic conferences can be a nightmare of face-name-badge-scanning. Twitter has changed this for many people. While Jessie once felt alienated at conferences, she's found that connecting with people on Twitter has transformed the hallways of academic conferences into giant meet-ups where warm embraces replace dismissive face-name-badge scowls. For some people, the real strength of Twitter is its lightning speed. Reading Twitter updates when there is breaking news is like watching something unfold in real time. In terms of current events, there is no quicker way to find out what's happening. This may or may not be useful for scholars who have traditionally had the benefit of the long, slow, thoughtful response to the news of the day rather than the "hot take" that is popular now.

Still, Twitter can be an effective mechanism for academics to connect with other scholars, as we discussed in the previous chapter, and it can also be a way to help you connect with broader audiences. It's not simply a "megaphone" that can broadcast messages to big audiences. You can't just sign up one day and expect to have 150,000 followers the next (as Zeynep Tufekci does). Instead, think of Twitter as a way to extend your existing social networks and build relationships and connections with people you might not otherwise have a chance to meet in person.

For example, Jessie had been an admirer of Australian sociologist Deborah Lupton's work, but given that they live on different continents it was unlikely they would meet in person. When Jessie saw that Deborah had joined Twitter, she followed her, and they began a conversation that was little more than "Oh, I love your work. Glad to see you here. Look forward to seeing your updates." The connection on Twitter feels somewhat more "lightweight" than sending the same message via e-mail. Over a period of several years, they continued to connect using the "loose tie" of Twitter. Eventually, they met in person at an academic conference in the United Kingdom and are now collaborating on some research. The Twitter connection meant that when they met face to face in the United Kingdom their conversation was more fruitful and productive than it normally would have been. And, as they both returned to their homes on separate continents, they are able to maintain connections around their shared area of interest.

Twitter may also allow you a different kind of voice than your scholarly blog. When Jessie blogs at *Racism Review*, her voice is informal yet stays within the register of a serious scholar talking about serious matters. On Twitter, while she maintains the voice of a scholar-activist concerned about racial inequality, she may also talk about or share links about her love of documentary films and memoir writing, general writing advice, the latest news about transformations in higher education, cultural events in her city, and the occasional television show (#Scandal). This wider range of topics is closer to who Jessie is—concerned about racism to be sure, but able to talk about a wide range of other things as well. When people see and interact with this more multidimensional voice on Twitter, they may be more likely to read something longer like a blog post or a *New York Times* op-ed. Twitter is a way to build an audience, but it doesn't work in a very straightforward, instrumental way.

Twitter can be difficult for many of us to really understand at first. Howard Rheingold describes many of the things that make Twitter a compelling online space for some: openness, immediacy ("a rolling present"), variety, reciprocity, and community forming. But he also says that "it's clear that many of the people I talk to about it just don't get why anyone wastes their time with it. So I tell them that to me, successful use of Twitter comes down to tuning and feeding." In other words, if you want to gain real value—useful information, answers to questions, new friends and colleagues—out of the time you spend on Twitter, then you have to know how both "tune the network of people you follow, and how to feed the network of people who follow you," Rheingold says.[20]

Figuring out who to follow so that your timeline is filled with interesting information and people can take some time. Hashtags and lists are often good places to look for key people that you want to follow. In terms of how to "feed the network of people who follow you," think about what people get out of following you. Are you adding something of value to other people's timelines? One of the best ways for academics to become familiar with Twitter, find people to follow, and gain followers is through conferences that are using hashtags.

Conferencing

The Twitter "back channel" can enliven conferences by enabling additional conversations among people using a conference hashtag. People use a particular hashtag (any word or set of letters and numbers with a # symbol in front of it) to preface their comments. For example, #ASA15 becomes a hashtag for the annual sociology conference. Individuals can follow conversations at a particular conference even if they didn't get to attend in person—a tremendous boon for those with intellectual curiosity and limited travel budgets.

For academics who toil in relative isolation from others who share their immediate interests, the social connection of Twitter back channels can also provide an opportunity to curate the ideal academic department. In another era, scholars may have identified strongly with their PhD-granting university, their undergraduate college or university, or the academic department in which they are currently employed. The rise of social media permits one to create a new arrangement of colleagues. Social media researcher Bonnie Stewart's investigation into scholarly practices with Twitter refers to the interactions there as "networked scholarship."[21] Stewart found that networked scholarship rewarded connection, collaboration, and curation among individuals, rather than roles or institutions.

This broadened view of scholarship emphasizes public ties and public discussions. Scholars now have conversations via Twitter and blogs and maintain close collegial ties with others who share their scholarly interests—even though they may not share an institutional home or academic department. Today, rather than being restricted to the colleagues we find in our own department, scholars (and teachers) go online to find intellectual companionship, in effect, curating the ideal academic department and tailoring it to their interests.

LinkedIn

Some people have described LinkedIn as a "professional, buttoned down version of Facebook," and that's a fair description. Like an institutional web page, it can lend you some professional credibility. It also has built-in capacity for blogging. Perhaps one of the most useful features on LinkedIn is its groups. For example, if you wish to curate news and information about a particular topic, and connect with others who are interested in the same topic, LinkedIn gives you the option to create a group around that topic.

In 2009, Paul Sonnier, who describes himself as a strategy consultant and social entrepreneur based in La Jolla, California, created a LinkedIn group around his interest in digital health. He posts the latest news on this topic, and other members in the group can post things there, too—but only news related to digital health (no cat videos allowed). Today, that group has over thirty-six thousand members. Media outlets frequently contact Sonnier when they are looking for an expert on digital health. Given that LinkedIn is frequently used by those outside academia, this may be an especially pertinent resource for graduate students and others considering careers outside of academia.

ResearchGate, Academia.edu, and Open Access Repositories

These platforms do much the same thing, with very slight differences: they provide space for academics to upload papers. Other researchers can find and "follow" you, and you can tag—or add on—co-authors and collaborators. Most importantly, as a researcher, you can also find work that is typically hidden behind pay walls or otherwise inaccessible, and, as a public scholar, these sites make your research discoverable. Academia.edu provides metrics about how many times a paper of yours has been downloaded, when someone searched for your work, and what paper they found. These are entertaining, but their value is still a bit murky (more on metrics in chapter 7). The main difference between ResearchGate and Academia.edu, other than metrics, seems to be that ResearchGate tends to have more people from the biological sciences, technology, and related disciplines, whereas Academia.edu tends to have more scholars from the social sciences and humanities. To be clear, both are commercial platforms and free to use for the time being, but some academics have raised concerns about these sites monetizing academic work. This hasn't happened yet, but many think it will only be a matter of time. Instead of these commercial sites, academics can use their own institutional repositories or other noncommercial open access repositories to make their work available to the public. There are hundreds of not-for-profit scholarly repositories; you only need to choose one. For a comprehensive list, check the Directory of Open Access Repositories (http://www.opendoar.org/).

Tumblr, Pinterest, Instagram

Let's say that you are doing research on the ways the marketing of toys is gendered, and specifically on the "pink" and "blue" labeling of toys, for your dissertation. You may want to start a Tumblr that is simply about the issue of gendered marketing of these products. While Tumblr is called a blogging platform, it's very visual, and often the kinds of blog posts you see there are images rather than long blocks of text—although those are there, too. Like Pinterest, which is comprised only of images, and Instagram, which consists of images with a little bit of text, Tumblr is really well suited for collecting and curating research that is visual.

You could use Tumblr to post examples of what you're studying, like the ways toys are marketed differently to boys and girls. While you could also use Pinterest or Instagram to do this, the advantage of Tumblr is that it will also connect you to other people who share this interest, and they'll post examples that you might not have seen. In other words, Tumblr is a great platform for sharing niche interests.

The people you connect with on Tumblr who share your fascination with the gendered marketing of products for children will be a likely audience for what you write later. (We'll discuss more about how to build your audience in chapter 5.) There's no one right tool for your work, and there's no need to feel compelled to sign up for all of these tools. Play around. Experiment. See what works for you and where the people are that you wish to connect with, and then go there.

Facebook

Many people are beginning to see Facebook as an increasingly problematic social media platform for several reasons. Those who live under repressive political regimes have been placed in physical danger when they are required to use their government-issued name, which makes them easier to locate and lock up. Facebook's algorithm boosts business advertisements over social messaging. There's a lot of evidence to suggest that Facebook is on the wane with younger users; in fact, the largest demographic of new users are those sixty-five and older. That said, it's a bit of a behemoth with over 1.9 billion users (as of this writing), which makes it hard to ignore if you want to reach a wide audience.

If you wish to use Facebook, set up a page that is focused on your research, and that is separate from your personal page. If you're interested in the gendered marketing of toys, for example, you may want to occasionally post links to news stories about that topic on your Facebook page. For example, when the chain store Target recently announced that they were no longer going to organize the toy section of their stores by gender, you could have posted an article, or several articles, about that news on your research page. Then, once you've finished the research and begin to put together your book proposal, you can include the number of followers you have, your platform, in your book proposal to a publisher. Once you get the book contract, and have a title, cover art, and a release date, you can convert the marketing-gender-in-children's-products interest page into your book's page. That way, the people who have been following your updates on this topic with interest will know about your new book.

What you don't want to do is leave creating the Facebook page to the very end of this process: it can feel like spam, or unwanted advertising, and be just generally icky. For example, an acquaintance of Jessie's, whom she'd met at conferences a couple of times, asked to "friend" her on Facebook. She thought, "oh, how nice, she wants to connect." And then, about thirty seconds after accepting the friend request, Jessie received a subsequent request asking her to "like" her new book page. Personally, Jessie was put off by that request because she realized that the friend request was designed to send her to that book page, and she was therefore much less interested in all that the author had to say—it seemed like unsolicited advertising. Since there was something inorganic about the way the author friended her, Jessie was less likely to reshare what she had to say.

So, if you decide you want to use Facebook for your work, be sure to set up a Facebook page for your book organized around the subject of your research well in advance of the book's release date.

Managing Your Time

How much time, you ask, will all of this take? Won't using social media be a major time waster? The answer is that it will take as much or as little time as you wish to give to it. Creating your own website, and blogging, could take a couple of hours or a full workweek. It's a bit like teaching, or writing: it will expand to fill the time you allow it. "It doesn't take as much time as people think—but it's true, there are only 24 hours in the day," says Zeynep Tufekci about how she manages being a public scholar. "There's definitely a time cost to it, but I'm not doing it at the expense of tenure but I am doing it at the expense of publishing more. I could have done more peer-reviewed articles if I hadn't been engaged in public scholarship, but that's the path I've taken."

Our advice is to start slowly and pick just one thing to begin with, such as blogging. Once you're comfortable with using that one piece of social media, you can then move on to something else. You may decide to use the preceding list as a kind of road map. Start by establishing your own domain name, then move down the list of social media tools.

What we've presented is by no means a comprehensive set of social media tools. There are other great resources out there that we haven't discussed, which have large user-bases, and that are being used effectively by scholars to engage with people beyond the academy about intellectual work. Some of these tools will also come and go. Twitter and Facebook may be the next Friendster, LiveJournal, or DiaryLand, all of which failed in the social media marketplace. It's not the individual tools that are magic; it's how they enable you to connect with other people. Digital tools just make that easier and faster than our previous analog practices. The good news is that once you learn one tool, that knowledge translates into how to use other tools. To feel comfortable using different tools, you need to be digitally fluent.

Digital Fluency for Academics

Reading this chapter, you may be thinking, "Digital tools are fine for other people, but I'm hopelessly behind, out-of-the-digital-loop, old, or simply unable to learn this stuff." How do you, dear reader, get on the other side of the digital turn? There are lots of resources available for you, and we've gathered some of the best ones for you here. Take what is useful and leave the rest for another time.

> *Net Smart* by Howard Rheingold. This is actually two resources in one: the book, *Net Smart*, and Howard Rheingold himself. The book is a primer on social media and all things digital. It is useful for undergraduates who are supposedly "born digital," as well as for those of us born long before the rise of the popular Internet. Rheingold (www.rheingold.com) is an autodidact, Internet guru,

and honorary sociologist. He's sometimes referred to as a futurist, but it's probably better to say that he's just damn prescient about what's coming down the road about how we use technology. In 1993, he wrote *Virtual Community*, easily twenty years ahead of its time in describing and predicting how people were connecting online. And, in 2002, long before a majority of people in the United States had smart phones, he wrote *Smart Mobs*, a book that talked about the way that mobile technology was the "next frontier." True to form, he has lots of interesting ideas about teaching with and about digital technology. He's posted a series of videos, which you can find here: http://clalliance.org/rheingold/. If the digital turn is new for you, think of Howard as your avuncular guide. He's always interesting, worthwhile, and very likely spot on about what's next in digital technologies.

Lynda.com. Even the most tech savvy among us need to learn new things. When Cathy Davidson was putting together her Future of Higher Ed online course, she had little time and a tiny budget, but she needed to figure out how to make digital videos, edit them, and get them uploaded to the course site. So she and a student assistant studied Lynda.com. "We couldn't have done the FuturesEd project without Lynda.com," she said. Whether you go to Lynda.com or just search online through the whole vast web for what you want to know, it's very likely that someone, somewhere—bless their hearts—has made a video tutorial that will teach you what you want to learn in step-by-step fashion. This is the "gift economy" of the web at its most useful.

Find your nearest educational technologist or digital librarian. Today, most institutions of higher ed have at least one person on staff who has a job title that is something like "educational technologist" or "digital librarian." These are very helpful human beings to know. You should seek them out, buy them coffee, chat them up, and see what they have on offer. They may well be creating workshops with you in mind.

Find a tech-savvy friend, and hang out. You may have heard of "hackathons," which are really just opportunities for people to casually learn about technology in close proximity to each other. There is often beer and pizza involved—backed up by science. The way that people learn technology best (and, some would say, learn just about anything best) is by learning it from a friend, or in the currently popular phrase, "the guide at the side." When Jessie first started working at a job that required an hour-long train ride, she was very fortunate to have an academic colleague, Chris Toulouse, who rode the same train to a job in the same department, who happened to be very tech savvy. Those conversations with Chris sparked Jessie's interests, guided her wanderings, and helped her hone many of the questions she had about these new technologies. Occasionally, they would get together, drink beer, and poke around the computer, but mostly they just talked about the kinds of tech stuff they were both interested in. That was 1995, and that friend made all the difference for Jessie's quest to learn about technology. So, find the geeky person nearby, hang out with them, and buy them a beer.

Organize an event or Meetup. So, you've read *Net Smart*, poured through Lynda.com videos, located a nearby ed tech specialist, and found a geek-buddy. Take the next step: organize an event at your institution. Perhaps you want to invite Howard Rheingold (or some other Internet guru) to speak at your institution. You could invite colleagues interested in technology to have coffee during the common hour. Or you could use the platform Meetup .com to organize or find a group of people interested in a particular aspect of technology, say podcasting, for an in-person group meeting.

Conclusion

The digital turn in academia is transforming how we go about the routine, everyday tasks of scholarly work. So far, these changes make a lot of our work easier (think of the always-available library resources online) and also more expansive (the seemingly endless stream of e-mails to be answered). The digital turn is also changing how we approach being a public scholar. For those who are looking to build an audience beyond a small circle of academic peers, an ever-growing array of tools offer the potential for a wider reach. If you're new to all that is digital, start small, with something you feel comfortable doing, and build from there.

... 5 ...

Building an Audience

For Alondra Nelson, the process of building an audience for her book began years before it was written. "Because several of the key figures in the account I tell in *Body and Soul* had become distrustful of researchers and reporters," Nelson says, "I had to spend years building trust with my informants." This meant attending events and social gatherings, or showing up at workshops and meetings that, on the face of it, had little to do with the history of the Black Panther Party she was writing. It was necessary, she says, because the group of men and women who were members or allies of the Black Panthers in the 1960s and 1970s were a key audience for Nelson.[1]

Using social media was a no-brainer for Nelson since it was "already a way she interacted with the world." It became a way she shared with friends and colleagues news about the progress of the book, and later, the book tour. Nelson started a listserv in 1998, and began to cultivate relationships with people who were subjects and potential audiences for her book. Because she has longstanding relationships with people on a variety of platforms, she can "say to

Facebook friends and Twitter followers, 'Hey, I've got this book coming out and I'm really excited about it,' without feeling like a used car salesperson." These are relationships she hopes to have for years, new book or not.

As Nelson's experience suggests, building an audience for your work can take years, and many different forms. Many academics commonly assume that they can "come onto social media two weeks before they have a book coming out." But it doesn't work that way. "It's the longevity of these relationships and the density of the personal networks built over time that make social media useful," Nelson says. Alongside her personal Facebook account, she created a Facebook page for her book project and used it to share archival materials she uncovered during her research, especially photographs of the Black Panther Party's health activism. She also used the Facebook page as a way to share news about publication dates and reviews of the book, and as a way for people who were interested in her work to reach out to her.

Social media made it easier for potential audiences to find and contact Nelson about her work. It was a "much more approachable way" to contact her than writing to her Columbia University e-mail account, she explains. For some individuals, a mention of her book on social media was the first time they had ever heard of the Black Panther Party. It led to speaking engagements at colleges and universities, at bookstores, as well as at small community-based venues filled with nonacademics and a new generation of activists who were more social media savvy. This multifaceted strategy for building an audience worked for Nelson because she was clear about her goals. She needed the book to meet the standards for tenure, and she wanted to reach multiple audiences that included both academics and activists across several generations. The sociologist's hard work paid off: she was promoted and, at last count, *Body and Soul* won over thirty book awards from academic associations as well as community-based organizations.

Clarify Your Goals

"Before you jump in, have a goal in mind," advises Nate Palmer, who created a popular online teaching guide, *Sociology Source* (www .sociologysource.org), and now leads workshops for other academics. When people seek him out for advice, Palmer says they often aren't clear on what their goals are for using social media, like blogging, to expand their audience. "When people say to me, 'I want to start a blog for my research.' I always reply, 'Great! But, why do you want to blog about your research? Imagine that your blog gets you 100% of your desired audience. Now that you have their attention, what do you want to do with it?'" It's important to know what your goals are because then "it's easier to identify what you should be talking about and how you should frame your discussions," Palmer suggests.[2]

So, consider the contribution you would like your work to make. Knowing your goals and having a clear understanding of where you want to go can make all the difference in how you build an audience. If you are clear about your goals, you can find your audience, and they can find you. Is your goal to land a tenure-track job, or be promoted within the one you already have? Is your goal to spark a social movement, or, perhaps more modestly, to influence policy makers to make a change you've identified as necessary in your work? Do you want to be known as one of a handful of experts on your subject area? Or is your goal is some combination of all of these? Let's take each of these goals in turn.

"Prior to tenure, I tended to think of my audience as the tenure committee," says Dustin Kidd. If your main goal is to secure a tenure-track job, or be promoted in the tenure-stream job you already have, then your focus should be on publishing peer-reviewed journal articles and scholarly monographs. As the coin of the realm in academia, you will need to publish journal articles and books in order to succeed as a university-based scholar. Kidd concedes that while thinking of your tenure committee as your audience may be less than ideal, "institutional pressures push many of us to think that way." It can be hard to shake these pressures, even post-tenure. Although Kidd did the research for his book *Pop Culture Freaks* right after being promoted, he says, "I still had that mindset."[3]

Success in the traditional academic realm can offer scholars the credibility to launch a more widely visible career as a public intellectual at more senior stages of their careers. But for some people, building a large audience happens along the way to other goals. For example, Lisa Wade started the *Sociological Images* blog in 2007 as a teaching resource for herself and a handful of her friends. She was one year out of graduate school and all the people she'd TA'd with in grad school were spread out all over the country, so it was a way to keep in touch with them, says Wade. While she thought that the audience would be her pals from graduate school, maybe a few other graduate students, and some sociology professors, "that's not how it turned out." Today, while a large percentage of the hundreds of thousands of regular readers, about 80 percent, she estimates, are not involved in sociology, they enjoy her image-driven insights about the social world.[4] Wade's success in building an audience for her blog also led to a book contract with a trade press.

Her social media following of 125,000 or 130,000 individuals made her more attractive to editors. But it was the discipline of blogging regularly that really helped, she says. "The fact that I've written 3,000 blog posts in the last eight years [means that] I am probably better at writing for a general audience than I would be if I hadn't written 3,000 blog posts." Writing for a general audience "is a skill that requires a lot of practice, and practice is putting in the time. . . . Eight years of daily writing has helped me so much," Wade says.

For some scholars, building an audience is part of a larger effort to politically mobilize people. Legal scholar Michelle Alexander's book *The New Jim Crow: Mass Incarceration in the Age of Colorblindness* analyzes rising rates of imprisonment in the United States. In exacting detail, Alexander enumerates elements of case law, legal precedent, and established practice that insure that African Americans, especially African American young men, fill the growing number of jail and prison cells built for them. The fact that more African Americans are under correctional control—in prison or jail, on parole or probation—than were enslaved in 1850 is evidence, she argues, that we never eliminated the racial caste system in America known as Jim Crow. We merely redesigned it.

But Alexander doesn't end with this damning critique. This new racial caste system is built on mass incarceration, and can never be dismantled without a major social movement to demand radical change, she says. Such a movement is possible, she contends.[5] In interviews, the author has been candid about her desire to see the book spark such a movement, as well as about the public's initial lack of interest in her book. From the outset, Alexander has been clear about her goals, working diligently to create interest and build an audience for the book and, ultimately, for the movement she hopes to foment.

Michelle Alexander is an example of someone who is widely recognized for her work as a scholar, and who is regularly consulted by a variety of media outlets on her area of expertise. Still, some suggest that the era of the public intellectual may be over, and that most would-be public intellectuals in the United States can only hope to attract a small audience at best. Sociologist George Ritzer's term "McDonaldization" is now part of the public lexicon, and his book on that topic has sold more than two hundred thousand copies (and been translated into fifteen languages). Ritzer doesn't consider himself a public intellectual because, he says, he is "rarely contacted by the American media." When he is contacted, "it is usually by small local radio stations or newspapers."[6]

Here, we might disagree with Ritzer and argue that he has already achieved the goal of being a public intellectual since the term he coined is well known, and his book is widely read. Still, the fact that Ritzer has achieved this level of success and yet does not see himself as a public scholar illustrates the importance of clarifying your goals so that you know when you've reached them. Ritzer raises an important issue about how we measure success, when he writes, "the very nature of success in the academic world militates against success in the public realm."[7] He urges disciplines to transform institutional reward structures to recognize the achievements of those who succeed as public social scientists (see more on this in chapter 7).

But academia may not be the place where your goals take you. If you are set on making a difference in a particular policy area, then your work may have a somewhat different focus. If your goal is to be recognized as "the expert" on a particular subject, your strategy for building an audience will vary according to whom you want to recognize your expertise. If you mainly want recognition from academic peers, then you should focus on more traditional routes of publishing. If, however, you want to be recognized across multiple audiences as the expert on your subject, then you will have to find out where those audiences—or "networks," or "tribes"—are already gathering.

Find out what and where your audience reads. If your goal as a public scholar is to influence your local school board election, then you should try to reach those who will be voting in that election. Since they probably read your local newspaper or neighborhood blog, you might start there. If, on the other hand, your goal is to reach the audience of regular readers at the *New York Times*, you might start paying attention to what's in the news.

Using News Hooks

Writing op-eds is a popular way for scholars to reach new audiences. However, getting op-eds published can be challenging. Zeynep Tufekci, who is now a monthly contributor to the *New York Times* opinion pages, started out by pitching an op-ed. "I had an idea in mind about a blog post I wanted to write, but instead of doing that, I sent a pitch to the editor, and they published it," she says. "I don't think academics pitch enough." Though we discussed op-eds in chapter 2, they are worth mentioning again here because they can be an effective way of building your audience—and can quickly get your name associated with an issue for a much larger readership. However, op-eds must be timely in order for newspapers to publish them.

There are several key things to keep in mind for what makes an item "newsworthy" in the eye of editors. The one to keep uppermost in your mind is, what is the "news hook" for the piece I want to pitch? If you are pitching an op-ed to an editor, they will want to know that the piece relates to the news cycle they are operating within. There are ways to navigate the different timelines of academic research and journalism. Sometimes, your work suddenly becomes relevant through no effort of your own. When Tufekci pitched her second op-ed to the *Times*, she says, "I wanted to write about Twitter and social movement organizing, that it has a boom, bust cycle which makes it challenging to make these movements last. That's an interesting academic question that I thought would also be interesting to a general audience, but there was no news hook." Then, events intervened.

"The day I published that, the government in Turkey banned Twitter literally within hours of my piece going online. So, suddenly this was a hot issue that a lot of people were paying attention to." In this case, the news hook happened after the piece came out, but you can't count on the timing of world events. More commonly, you have to be ready to react to world events and pitch to editors in response to events. Of course, news organizations today exist in a media ecosystem where they are eager for their authors and readers alike to share their content through social media channels. And, having a social media presence, particularly through a scholarly blog and Twitter, can mean that the *New York Times* reaches out to you when there is breaking news relevant to your research.

The audience Tufekci is now able to reach has changed since she first went online as a scholar. "Early on, my audience was my academic friends." Then, as she started blogging and as things were happening in Turkey that were relevant to her area of research interest, more journalists tuned in. Then, people started linking to her because she was in Gezi Park when the protests there were happening.

Text Box 5.1 News Hooks

When you pitch an idea to an editor, they will want to know what the "hook" is—how does it tie in to what their readers want to know?

- Impact—Is this something that will affect thousands, maybe even millions of people? If so, include this as part of your pitch.
- Conflict—Is there a sharply opposing view from yours? Or are you expressing a view that's in stark contrast to a widely held belief? Conflict is often a news hook; the *New York Times*' "Room for Debate" is structured in this way.
- Prominence—Are there well-known people involved? Include their names and how they are involved near the top of your pitch.
- Timeliness—Is there something happening in the news that connects to your research? Make that clear.
- Proximity—Every news organization wants to feature material that's of interest to local readers. Is there a local angle to your pitch?
- Novelty—There is an aphorism in journalism: dog bites man—not news; man bites dog—news! Is there something novel or unique about what you've found?

She also has friends around the world. "My audience," she says, "is an accumulation of all those [groups]."

Even if you're not a world traveler, or lucky enough to land your work in the *New York Times*, news hooks can still work to your advantage for building an audience. If you have a blog, you can write a post about a news item or current event that is related to your work. Similarly, if you are on Twitter, you may want to share updates about your work in real time as a news event unfolds. "Jump into conversations about news items that you know about," advises Letta Wren Page, who works with the *Society Pages*, a host and aggregator of several academic blogs (including *Sociological Images*). "If there's a big story on gun control, check out that hashtag on Twitter and get in there. If you have the perfect graph to tell a story or a list of facts at your fingertips, put them out into the public." Today when news breaks, the general public and a good number of journalists from major outlets turn to Twitter. So if you can contribute to a trending hashtag, your work may have a better chance of being seen. "Writing the 140-character-including-your-link version of your research is the new elevator pitch," suggests Page.[8]

Sometimes building an audience isn't about tapping into the news cycle; instead, it means creating a new set of readers from seemingly disparate worlds.

Connecting Different Audiences

A number of years ago, fellow graduate students Nathan Jurgenson and P. J. Rey discovered they had a mutual interest in social theory and the Internet. But when they looked around, they were frustrated. "It was tough to get theory people to talk about the Internet and even more difficult to get the tech-researchers to take theorizing seriously, especially that which isn't strictly instrumental," Jurgenson says.[9] So they decided to organize a conference, which they called Theorizing the Web, bringing together scholars, artists, and even high-tech professionals to reflect, think, talk, and have a good time. The conference was so successful that it became an annual event. The gatherings enabled them to build a public presence for theoretical work on the emerging digital world.

What Jurgenson and Rey did was to create a new audience by identifying a unique intersection of interests, "social theory" and "the Internet." This strategy for building an audience is right in line with what one does to establish oneself as a scholar. That is, you need to articulate a theme and produce work around it, and then connect with others doing related work both online and in face-to-face meetings, typically at conferences.[10] The theme should be one that few, if any, other people have identified. Sometimes, this involves bridging two already established areas and then organizing a series of conferences around that theme, like Jurgenson and Rey did with social theorizing and emerging technologies. Through those conferences, they created an audience for their work, and in the process they created a following among those who were interested in thinking theoretically about the Internet and digital technologies.

"Our goal was really to build community that we didn't find ready-made elsewhere," Rey says. "We thought an exciting conference would try to get past the jargon and focus on ideas important to a wide audience." The first Theorizing the Web conference introduced him to a number of other scholars with whom he now regularly collaborates. "For me, these relationships were the primary motivator in turning this original conference into an annual event."

The *Sociological Cinema*, a popular teaching resource site, created an audience where there was none by identifying a unique intersection: the vast world of online videos and the college instructors who want short, teachable multimedia elements to use in the classroom. It was created by Lester Andrist and a few friends, who realized, while they were still in graduate school, there was a huge unmet need for a kind of online clearinghouse for digital video.[11] When they launched the *Sociological Cinema*, Andrist says, "we were early subscribers to the idea that if you build it, your audience *won't necessarily come*." This is a common mistake that many academics make. Even if you identify a unique intersection that you want to cultivate, and you have a digital presence, it doesn't necessarily mean that you will get the audience you desire. "You have to put energy into making your content visible," Andrist advises. "It is perfectly possible to build an amazing and thoughtful website, but if you don't find creative ways to put your site on people's radars, it will languish in the less illuminated corners of the Internet."[12]

In order to avoid the fate of languishing in dark corners of the Internet, Andrist says he and his colleagues worked hard at "getting the word out about new posts and resources. This involves meeting people where they're at," Andrist explains. "All of our friends were on Facebook, so that seemed like a logical place to create a presence." Eventually, they expanded their outreach to include a Twitter account, Pinterest boards, and a Tumblr. "As we learned the ropes of each platform, it became clear that each had distinct competencies. In other words, the posts that got attention on Facebook, didn't necessarily get much attention elsewhere," Andrist says. However, on each of these platforms, the audience they were trying to reach was the same: college instructors interested in video pedagogy.[13]

Despite popular misconceptions about digital technology, it's never possible to reach a wide audience "with just one click." Building an audience takes work and time. And it's worth acknowledging that the very term "audience" may be on its way to obsolescence in the digital era.[14] Whether you think of your readers as an audience, tribe, community, collaborators, or a fan base, consider cultivating relationships with them over a long period of time and in a reciprocal conversation rather than sending a one-time blast of information about your project, book, or website.

The (False) Promise of Analytics

Analytics are the data that's generated automatically by digital media platforms. These days, there's a tremendous amount of hyperbole about analytics and what they can do, often driven by marketing firms promising to "deliver customers" and "increase return on investment" for businesses. But this kind of marketing logic doesn't translate well to the world of building an audience for scholarly ideas. "Analytics tell you how popular something was, but not *why* something was popular," Nate Palmer explains.[15] Palmer says that while he pays attention to a variety of measures, such as Google analytics and the analytics provided by Facebook and Twitter, he doesn't "allow them to affect what I write." What works in one post isn't that easy to replicate. "In the past when I have tried to emulate the characteristics of a popular post, they have rarely paid off the second time."

Becoming known as a public scholar through digital media is sometimes referred to as "building your brand." This rankles most academics as it smacks of the commercialization of ideas, which at times can be highly problematic. However, by building your audience, and becoming known for a particular area of research, you are simply associating your name with an area of expertise. As Palmer explains his approach, "Within the first year, I had a clearly defined audience in my mind: Sociology 101 teachers. I looked into the data on who teaches 101 and found that it was disproportionately contingent faculty, graduate students, and early career faculty." By looking into the data, he knew that the people who would find his work most useful are those teaching the introductory course in his field, and he crafted the content there to meet the needs of his existing audience and attract a larger one.

Lisa Wade says she doesn't pay much attention to the analytics for her *Sociological Images* blog. "The only routine way I pay attention to the analytics is at the end of every month, I put up a, 'Here's how this month looked' post." She says she also checks Facebook for the post that got the most "likes," and then, she'll post something there telling readers which post of hers got the most "thumbs up" acknowledgments for the month, but "that's usually the extent to which I pay attention to analytics."[16] Still, some scholars find them valuable.

"I use analytics to get feedback on what I'm posting," says Lester Andrist. These give him "a sense of what works and what doesn't." While many people may rely on the number of likes a Facebook post gets or the number of re-tweets of a Twitter post in order to judge whether something was successful or well received, Andrist cautions that total numbers can be deceptive. "What is really important is the engagement rate," he says. The engagement rate is typically derived from some pretty basic math: how many people interacted with your post (liked or re-tweeted), divided by the larger number of how many people saw your post. As of this writing, both Facebook and Twitter currently offer this calculation for users within their platforms. Andrist says that by taking a little time each week to look at the engagement rate on posts from the *Sociological Cinema*, he's been able to increase it. By looking at the engagement rate he learned that when he shares a link, updates with photos almost always do better than ones without—the web is a visual medium—and he learned that the language describing the link affects whether people click on it. A humorous tie-in to a link will yield more engagement.

For example, a tweet with a URL that directs people to an article on Sigmund Freud might read, "#Freud's continuing relevance in social science," but that wouldn't do nearly as well as "This interesting post about #Freud's relevance will make you blush," even though the link is the same.

There's a cautionary tale about this that comes from the world of journalism. In a comparative study of French and American news websites, Angèle Christin observes that these sorts of web analytics now drive much of journalism. At many news websites, journalists toil in expansive rooms with counters on the walls displaying the "hits" news article received.[17] The number of hits on a particular piece of writing is sometimes tied to the number of clicks on each piece. The "upworthy" university, where only things with lots of likes and hits get discussed, is not a vision we would endorse (more about that in chapter 7). For most scholars, the promise of analytics for building an audience is at best modest and at worst false. Nate Palmer sums up the views of most academics when he says, "I only have so much time to dedicate to *Sociology Source*. I'd rather spend it figuring out what I want to say than figuring out which title is better click-bait."[18] In addition to being exhausting, the click-bait approach is antithetical to the relationship-building strategy we recommend. Building an audience through relationships may lead you to think about your audience as a number of distinct groups.

Segmenting Audiences

When Alondra Nelson was getting close to finishing work on her book about genetic ancestry testing and black political culture, she realized that she needed a different strategy when it came to discussing the book on social media. "My interests in science and technology can be quite technical—and frankly, all my friends don't share this passion!" she explains. Thus, she had to segment her audience. "I initially created *The Social Life of DNA* [Twitter] feed to spare my friends and colleagues—who aren't as interested as me in genetics, genetic ancestry testing, and the politics around science—from having to have these subjects in their timelines if they didn't want to read about them," Nelson says. Over time, this separate social media feed became part of the prepublication identity of the book.

Consider whether or not there is special messaging or specific language that would work better with a particular audience. Once he shook off the image of the tenure committee as his audience, Dustin Kidd says he was able to "actively think about very different audience groups who need to be engaged in different ways." For instance, he knows that there are scholarly peers, students, journalists, cultural influencers, policy makers, and a wider, general audience who all have different reasons why they might want to read his book about popular culture. Kidd says his awareness of multiple audiences, each with different levels of engagement, influences the way he uses social media to talk about his work. For example, when communicating with scholarly peers, "I focus on sharing newly released research (mine and especially others), funding opportunities, and links to debates related to academia." But he takes a different approach with journalists—a quick note, or observation, and a link to the research; and for students, both his students and students on other campuses, he prefers more informal discussions and debates online.[19] Students of all ages can also be an audience.

Earlier, we asked you to reflect on your goals for building an audience as a public scholar, and to think about how you want your work to make a contribution in the world. Depending on how you answered this question, you may want to build an audience by connecting with smaller civic or religious organizations or community groups. The authors of this book have both have participated in these kinds of events: Jessie has spoken at Christian pastoral staff meetings, Jewish community groups, and YWCA girls' empowerment groups; Arlene has spoken at churches, synagogues, and community organizations. They are not alone, of course.

African American studies scholar Imani Perry situates her own work in the tradition of late-nineteenth and mid-twentieth-century

African American intellectuals who engaged in public life in a multitude of ways, such as participating in civic organizations, churches, and professional societies. In reflecting on her own engagement as a public intellectual, Perry writes:

> I recently spent an afternoon with girls at an urban high school in Philadelphia that serves a largely black, poor, and working-class community. I am frequently invited to speak to young people, usually girls. I talk to them about academic success and offer some words of motivation. This group of girls had a stunning combination of brilliance and need. I spoke about my personal history and we discussed their interests, and our mutual inspirations. It was a different kind of public-intellectual experience. Around the same time, I gave interviews that were quoted in newspapers in the United States and Britain. Guess which "public intellectual" work felt more meaningful? I'm not suggesting that everyone would take teenagers over the *New York Times*, but if I had to choose, I certainly would.[20]

Perry's comments speak to the importance of reflecting on the kind of difference you want to make in the world with your scholarship. There is, as she notes, so much work to be done on a wide range of issues, including incarceration, public health, political representation, unemployment, and educational inequality. If your goal is to connect with much younger audiences, like the teenagers Perry mentions here, then you're unlikely to reach them by publishing op-eds in the *New York Times*.

Perry's strategy represents a different kind of audience building, one that is unlikely to increase the number of books you sell or the audience for your peer-reviewed articles to a great extent. This kind of public engagement as a scholar is really about doing the work of translating your academic research into a language that's accessible to the widest possible audience. This does not mean sacrificing scholarly gravitas, rigorous social science methodology, or the value of peer review. Rather, it means rethinking the kinds of questions you are asking with your research, which audience you want to reach with it, and what kind of difference you want to make.

Scholars and Policy Makers

Scholars working within the tradition of participatory action research tend to think of audience members as collaborators in the research. Academics Brett Stoudt and Maria Torre partnered with mothers in the South Bronx to create the Morris Justice Project. The women in the South Bronx neighborhood had already begun to film police interactions with their sons, using their cell phones to document regular harassment, when Stoudt and Torre approached them to be coresearchers. "The project was intentionally designed to deeply engage a small section of NYC in order remain local and focused on just one neighborhood," says Stoudt. Even though they focused on just one section of the Bronx, their work has had broad influence. "Our research findings and products made their way into the city-wide campaign for police-reform, and at times into the hands of lawmakers," says Torre, and "each instance is grounded in the community from which the data was produced."[21] When the findings from their project made it into the hands of lawmakers, they had to communicate in a way that lawmakers understand. And that's often very different from a standard, peer-reviewed journal article.

Drug policy expert Julie Netherland moved from traditional academic training into policy advocacy work. In order to get policy makers' attention as an audience, Netherland says, "You have to tell a compelling story to help personalize an issue and highlight the human costs, then connect that to your research." Without this, policy makers have no reason to act. Even with a compelling personal narrative backed up by research, lawmakers may not respond. Whether at the local, state, or federal level, when thinking about building your audience among policy makers, Netherland says it is important to connect with people in organizations who are already doing this work, who have given the policy issues a lot of thought. Some organizations will help you craft or place an op-ed in major news outlets.[22] If you're unsure of how to connect with advocates, there are some organizations that work as a kind of "matching" service between scholars and policy makers (see box 5.2).

Conclusion

Academics do not spend a great deal of time thinking about building audiences for their work. That's the job of marketing people at publishing houses, we tell ourselves. Books are, and will remain, important in the digital age, to be sure. Few of us will publish that big crossover book, however. But the proliferation of online media is good news for academics who wish to reach wider audiences. Online media offer us many more opportunities to speak to people outside of the ivory tower. At the same time, there has never been a noisier, more competitive time to try to reach a general audience with one's research. The challenge today is how to break through this noise and find your audience.

By starting with a clear set of goals about what you wish to accomplish by becoming a public scholar, you can develop the appropriate skills, tools, and collaborators to reach those who will most appreciate your work. There is a range of options for building your audience, depending on what your goals are. For those who are most interested in a traditional route to tenure, promotion, and a public audience, focusing on peer-reviewed articles and scholarly monographs should be your top priorities; yet even these traditional forms of academic publishing can be more discoverable online, and, in turn, more widely cited by academic colleagues. If you are more interested in connecting with more varied audiences, then community groups may be the place you want to focus your attention. If, on the other hand, your primary goal is to influence policy makers around a particular issue, then you have to learn to tell a compelling story, backed by research, and collaborate with an advocacy group which is working on that issue already and see if there are ways to collaborate with them.

No matter what your goals are, the proliferation of digital technologies makes it possible to build audiences in ways that simply weren't fathomable earlier. Building your audience can take many different forms, but it is rarely instantaneous. Social media platforms are not simply megaphones for broadcasting messages to wider audiences; they are mechanisms for building networks and maintaining social ties. In the digital age, building the audience for your writing is fundamentally about expanding your networks, and that takes time. To determine what kinds of skills, tools, and platforms you will use to build your audience, you need to first clarify your goals for being a public scholar.

Before contacting a policy organization, academic researchers have typically done their research, but the process can also work the other way around. For example, scholars may ask what kind of research needs to be done to address specific policy needs, and then set about to do precisely that kind of research. Sociologist Harry Levine

Text Box 5.2 Influencing Policy

Scholar Strategy Network (http://www.scholarsstrategynetwork.org/)—If you want your research to influence policy, but don't know how to make those connections, you might consider applying to become part of the Scholar Strategy Network (SSN), which brings together leading scholars to address pressing public challenges at all levels. Scholars in the network prepare short, vividly written briefs highlighting their research findings and offering policy options about a wide range of issues. SSN scholars engage in consultations with policy makers in Washington, DC, and state capitals, and also work closely with advocates and leaders of citizen associations.

The Tobin Project (http://www.tobinproject.org/)—If you want to do research that fills a gap in policy making, you might contact the Tobin Project, which emphasizes "transformative research in the social sciences" and facilitates policy-scholar connections. The Tobin Project starts by identifying the gaps in research that might influence policy, and then finding scholars who want to engage policy by conducting original research that makes a contribution in this way. The project recently received a MacArthur Award for Creative and Effective Organizations, so it might be on to something.

---

had been doing his own research on marijuana arrests when he got involved with an advocacy organization and worked with them to produce a number of highly influential reports that highlighted racial disparities and fiscal waste entailed in marijuana arrests. Several news organizations, including the New York Times, featured some of Levine's research in a series of op-eds, such as "Whites Smoke Pot, but Blacks Are Arrested."[23] This combined scholarship and advocacy work eventually led to a six-part series in 2014 on marijuana legalization and an official editorial stance decrying the injustice of current marijuana laws, a rare move on the part of the New York Times. Armed with compelling personal narratives of severely disabled children whose only relief comes from medical marijuana, and backed by reams of research, Netherland and colleagues at the Drug Policy Alliance used the New York Times editorial stance to keep pressure on the state legislature. The same year that the six-part series ran, the New York State legislature approved the legalization of medical marijuana and Governor Cuomo signed it into law. Building an audience made it possible.

... **6** ...

The Perils of Going Public

A book about the hidden world of homosexuality among ostensibly "straight" guys caused quite a sensation. Straight white men frequently have sex with each other, Jane Ward argued in her book *Not Gay*—they just don't think of it as sex. Hazing rituals, homoerotic touching, and mutual masturbation sessions can't be reduced to latent homosexuality, or seen simply as evidence of nonsexual dominance and submission play, according to Ward. Heterosexual men, specifically white men, have sex with other men to affirm just how straight they are. Because of their privileges, white men have "more room to push sexual boundaries without being immediately pathologized."[1]

Ward received laudatory reviews in a variety of publications, approving tweets from a hunky male celebrity, and also hate mail, weird sexual propositions, confessional e-mails from straight men who wanted to share all the details of having sex with other men—and a great deal of abusive online commentary. But all the public attention began to wear on the author. The nasty comments and sexual propositioning seemed a bit like the Internet's version of someone shouting obscenities on a bus. While gratified that her book elicited so much discussion, Ward quickly tired of the negative onslaught, and stopped reading the feedback. Eventually, a friend offered to filter out the most offensive comments so that she would not have to read them and become upset, so that she could then focus on the ones that truly engaged with her work openly and charitably.

Most of us are happy to receive critical responses that are thoughtful and reasonable—it shows people are listening. But the rise of social media has also meant that our work travels into unknown spaces, in ways that we cannot always anticipate. That is, in many respects, a positive development: it means that our ideas have the potential today to circulate more broadly. But the ease with which ideas move through the world at lightning speed also introduces new risks. Producers of knowledge are vulnerable, particularly when our work challenges deeply felt assumptions about how the world works, and calls dominant groups to account—especially when we ourselves are members of less privileged groups, and we study dominant groups. The likelihood of getting into hot water is amplified if we write about highly politicized subjects.

Social media has introduced a whole new set of potential interlocutors—"trolls"—individuals who deliberately attack others online without engaging in reasonable debate. Lisa Wade often encounters them when she writes about gender and sexual politics at *Sociological Images*: "A lot of people have said things like 'I hope you get raped.'" Readers occasionally go to the trouble of googling her name to find out where she teaches, and then send her diatribes. Usually, she says, "they seem perfectly satisfied having had their say. 'Oh good, I called her a cunt 16 times, and now I feel better,'" and she rarely hears from them again. Once, though, a man kept sending her abusive e-mails. "Eventually, he ran out of steam and went away."[2] When Jessie wrote a short piece for the *New York Times* about the need to restrict online hate speech following the murder of nine black citizens at their church in Charleston, South Carolina, she received—ironically enough—lots of hateful speech, and even invitations to leave the country.

But sometimes harassment is not enough: a critic wishes to damage an individual's reputation, or even threaten their job. Black women academics seem particularly vulnerable to such attacks.[3] Saida Grundy's comments on Twitter about white men, race, and slavery in 2015 led a right-wing group that targets black women professors to launch an attack on her. Grundy had called white college males the "problem population" in America, posting, "Every MLK week I commit myself to not spending a dime in white-owned businesses. And every year I find it nearly impossible." She asked, "Can we just call St. Patrick's day the white people's Kwanzaa that it is?" A right-wing group culled several of the more provocative tweets and began a campaign to fire the newly appointed assistant professor at Boston University. Grundy apologized for "the position [she] put other people in" but was not yet an employee of the university when she produced the tweets in question.[4]

Grundy's upbringing shaped her worldview. In an earlier piece in *Essence*, she wrote about Aiyana Jones, a seven-year-old black girl shot and killed in a police raid in Detroit, near where Grundy lived at the time, which compared Jones's death to those of the girls who were murdered at the 16th Street Baptist Church in Birmingham, Alabama, in 1963. "The State does not protect little Black girls," she wrote.[5]

But she admits that she was "completely naïve" about Twitter. "I wanted to speak to a bubble [of like-minded people]. I was not trying for a mass conversation," Grundy said. "What I did not calculate was that there are people who hunt" for Twitter comments in order to stage coordinated attacks. Her experience suggests that while it's impossible to fully anticipate such attacks, before you say something publicly it is important to be mindful of the political landscape in which you operate. Grundy says that she didn't realize that the title of "professor," which suggests power and authority, made her a lightning rod for far-right attacks.[6]

Scholars intervene in debates when they publish work of direct relevance to policy discussions or social movements. Those who are activist-scholars may be less reticent about being at the center of conflicts than others, and may even see themselves engaged in producing knowledge that can be of use to activists engaged in contesting the powers that be. While some of us don't shy away from controversy, and sometimes we even court it, as a rule scholars tend to be wary of getting involved in fiery public debates. There's no sure way of guarding against the possibility of receiving unwanted attention if one goes public, but we can be aware of what some of the potential risks are, and be prepared for them should they occur.

Angry Subjects

Some time ago, a small town became embroiled in a bitter battle when a Christian right organization sponsored a ballot measure seeking to outlaw gay and lesbian civil rights. Families stopped their children from playing with those whose parents stood on the opposite side of the issue, and fist fights broke out over the matter in high schools. Why had sexuality become a central way people came to define themselves in these communities? Who supported these campaigns, and who opposed them? What could that tell us about the continuing resonance of homophobia, and about the fate of small communities in an era of globalization?[7]

Because she wanted to intervene in public debates about an issue of ongoing currency, Arlene wrote a book about these battles that was broadly accessible, hoping to elicit some attention, and perhaps cause conservative activists, and their supporters, to reflect upon the error of their ways. The book did receive attention—though not exactly the kind the author bargained for. It featured a few vivid portraits of local activists engaged in the conflict, including Christian conservatives as well as secular liberals. In keeping with the conventions of social science, she assigned pseudonyms to the subjects, and changed the name of the community where they lived. But when a newspaper published the real name of the town, in effect outing it, all hell broke loose. A copy of the book in which someone had crossed out the pseudonyms she had assigned to individuals and substituted individuals' real names began to make the rounds across town, and lots of people were upset.

The loudest objection came from one of the leaders of the conservative campaign, who cut a distinctive figure with her bouffant and heavy makeup. She charged the author with distorting their views, compromising her anonymity, and willful defamation. She even tried, unsuccessfully, to get the town to ban the book. The big-haired activist wrote a letter to the editor of the local newspaper describing herself as being the victim of a "hit and run" accident, and called upon the town to condemn the book for its supposed deceptions. Fortuitously, the author was about to move across the country to take another academic position just as the proverbial excrement hit the fan, but even that failed to diffuse the conflict, which carried on for several months.[8]

At least Arlene was not hung in effigy at the annual Fourth of July parade, like sociologists Arthur Vidich and Joseph Bensman, whose classic community study *Small Town in Mass Society* elicited the wrath of citizens of Candor, New York, when it was published in 1958. Vidich and Bensman's book exposed the political machinations of a clique of local businessmen who ran the town behind the facade of folksy democracy. Though the authors had changed the name of the town, the book outraged local residents, who charged them with compromising their anonymity and deceiving them about their motives.

While journalists use individuals' real names because they want to hold people accountable, academic social scientists tend to operate at greater remove in space and time. We analyze social patterns in the hope of understanding them better and contributing to the accumulation of scholarly knowledge. But by writing about contemporary issues we also have the capacity to intervene in ongoing social conflicts.

Arlene did not invite public scrutiny of her book *The Stranger Next Door* by her own subjects, but she didn't guard against it either. To get people to talk with her, and to fulfill institutional review board (IRB) requirements, she promised respondents that she would assign them pseudonyms and change the name of the town. Would this really provide them with sufficient cover, she wondered? Telling a good story often requires one to capture the individuality of people and a sense of place, and Arlene worried that the more she changed identifying characteristics, the less compelling the narrative would be. How could she capture a sense of her subjects' distinctiveness and still protect their privacy?

Taking a risk, she decided to vividly describe some defining characteristics of the town and of individual people in the book. As an activist-scholar, she wanted her book to play a role in producing knowledge and helping to diffuse what she saw as a senseless conflict. And she hoped, deep down, that by reading about themselves, activists on both sides—particularly those on the right—would come to think about the issues differently. With time the book did spark conversations that proved very useful in helping citizens to understand the source of the conflict, and how to move beyond it. Even the local fire chief praised it.

Generally speaking, we need to protect the anonymity of our informants, particularly as our IRBs require us to do so. But we should give the people we write about the chance to find out what we're saying about them. Some have suggested that open-access publication is the bare minimum required to enable laypeople to benefit from our research, and to criticize it if they wish. For example, when Benjamin Geer, a sociologist, published an open-access article in English on an activist group that campaigned for university autonomy in Egypt, he received immediate feedback from some of the participants in the study.[9] He wanted the article to be accessible to people in Egypt who don't read English, so he published an Arabic translation in an Arabic-language sociology journal, and he blogged about it in three languages. While Geer was gratified that the feedback he received was mainly positive, negative feedback is an ever-present possibility too—not only from the people we study, but also from our peers.

Social scientists expect measured, reasonable, and critical feedback, and we often even welcome it. Criticism is, after all, a vital component of creating a community of scholars and furthers the goal of developing social science knowledge. But when one's research is subjected to widespread scrutiny, the costs can be great. Being a public scholar online can mean stumbling in public.

Stumbling in Public

"Sometimes my pieces get 100,000 responses from readers . . . and they find *every* typo," says sociologist Zeynep Tufekci, who has written op-eds for the *New York Times* about protests in Turkey and elsewhere. You will make mistakes. If your work has a wide audience, more people will see your mistakes. This can be especially disconcerting for early career scholars.

Stumbling in public is not unique to scholars who use social media. It can happen to those who write books, too. For example, sociologist Alice Goffman wrote a book called *On the Run* based on an ethnographic study of "fugitive life in an American city," which we mentioned earlier (chapter 3). The book details the lives of several young black men living on "6th Street," a small intersection of a mostly black, poor neighborhood in Philadelphia. In addition to attracting widespread interest among sociologists, it also elicited a great deal of popular attention (including four reviews in the *New York Times*)—an unusual feat for a scholarly study.

Initial reviews were ecstatic; many regarded the book as a huge success. Cornel West endorsed it as "the best treatment I know of the wretched underside of neoliberal capitalist America." Writing in the *New York Times*, Alex Kotlowitz said it was "a remarkable feat of reporting" with an "astonishing" level of detail and honesty. The *New*

Yorker's Malcolm Gladwell called it "extraordinary," and Christopher Jencks predicted it would "become an ethnographic classic." But then a storm of criticism rolled in.

Some critics charged Goffman with white voyeurism, and with sensationalizing poverty. Dwayne Betts, who grew up in a neighborhood similar to the one that Goffman writes about, charged that *On the Run* pandered to stereotypes of black criminality. Betts placed the ethnography within what sociologist Victor Rios calls "the jungle book trope," a kind of self-aggrandizing fairy tale in which an innocent white person gets lost in the wild, is taken in by the wild people, survives, and returns to society with a story to tell.[10] Another critic charged that her ethnography did the opposite of what she intended. Rather than resist the forces of surveillance, "Goffman's revelation of black fugitive practices threatens to subject those communities to even more suffering."[11]

An anonymous critic, rumored to be an academic, penned a sixty-page, single-spaced diatribe that questioned her accuracy and methodology. Another published a scathing review that called Goffman's ethnography "implausible," likening her to the main character in the novel *Heart of Darkness*. "Like another entrepreneurial missionary, Conrad's Mr. Kurtz, she traveled into the heart of darkness, and while there, it seems that her methods became unsound."[12]

Most damningly of all, perhaps, Goffman was accused of legal and ethical misconduct. A legal ethics scholar, after fact-checking some of Goffman's sources, claimed that she had lied about some key interactions with Philadelphia's criminal justice system, and that by driving around with an armed man, an informant who was about to commit a murder, she was guilty of "conspiracy to commit murder under Pennsylvania law."[13] The fact that she had destroyed her field notes (to protect her informants, she said) only fueled the belief that she had something to hide. Goffman refuted many of these charges in a prominently placed interview in the *New York Times*, a luxury not often afforded to junior scholars.[14]

Writing a book that gets attention, and having a famous last name (Goffman's father was the eminent sociologist Erving Goffman), can make one more vulnerable. As academics, we learn to become social researchers in part by reading, analyzing, and criticizing the work of others. Clearly, Goffman made mistakes in the course of her research; most of us do at some point or other. But because the book received such wide acclaim and favorable initial attention, when criticisms surfaced they were also highly visible. Indeed, many of the criticisms lodged against Goffman seemed motivated, at least in part, by the outsized influence of her book.

Because the book moved out of the relatively protected world of academic sociology, and was read by journalists, criminal justice experts, and others, it was subjected to forms of scrutiny and accountability (such as fact-checking and legal verification) that few sociologists are forced to undergo. Chances are that if Goffman had a less famous lineage, or if her book hadn't received such over-the-top early reviews, it probably would have passed into the backlist of an academic press without much notice. As one of her chief critics conceded, "I would not be writing this review if *On the Run* were an ordinary academic book with similar flaws. Unlike most such books, however, *On the Run* promises to be very influential in academia and beyond, and it therefore demands closer attention."[15] Increased visibility means increased scrutiny, and that makes one more vulnerable to attack.

At times there is a fine line between being held accountable for one's views and being attacked for them. People who engage in critical analysis publicly, especially if they are making some kind of claim to being involved in social justice work, Lisa Wade says, can be hard on each other. Holier-than-thou critics have, at times, accused Wade of committing "symbolic violence" if they believe she is insufficiently attentive to the oppression of a particular group, or if her posts at *Sociological Images* can be construed as such. Wade says she is happy to be held accountable, and she "[tries] to be attentive to multiple sources of oppression." For example, when she posted a piece about drag queens, and two sociologists commented on it elsewhere in less-than-flattering terms, charging her with insensitivity, she was taken aback. But in the end, she says, "I don't really feel like it hurts me to acknowledge that a post wasn't perfect, or even that it was ignorant or hurtful" because, she says, "I want to learn" from others.[16]

Academics are not the only ones who eat our own, of course. When writer Ta-Nehisi Coates dubbed former Princeton professor and then regular MSNBC commentator Melissa Harris-Perry the foremost public intellectual in the United States, he was attacked by any number of people, including Dylan Byers, a reporter for *Politico*, who tweeted, "Ta-Nehisi Coates's claim that 'Melissa Harris-Perry is America's foremost intellectual' sort of undermines his cred, no?" Coates responded that Byers's dismissive reaction was a mark of the very "machinery of racism." Bitter public feuds such as these are, at times, about public posturing. Having a high profile can amplify the tendency for one to become a target. So can taking an unpopular political stand.

Academic Freedom and Administrative Backlash

In 2013, a public relations executive named Justine Sacco posted an offensive tweet to her account before she boarded a plane bound for South Africa. By the time her flight landed, that tweet had caused a furor, and she was fired from her job. A recent study in the United Kingdom found that one in ten job seekers between the ages of sixteen and thirty-four had been rejected for a job because of something posted on social media.[17] Though far less common in academia, some scholars have been suspended or fired from their jobs for their online remarks.

The same year as Sacco's controversial tweet, a lone gunman entered the Washington Navy Yard and opened fire, killing twelve people and seriously injuring three others. David W. Guth, a tenured professor of journalism at the University of Kansas, responded to the shootings on Twitter saying: "#NavyYardShooting The blood is on the hands of the #NRA. Next time, let it be YOUR sons and daughters. Shame on you. May God damn you." The University of Kansas suspended Guth, but later reinstated him when they determined that there was no official policy prohibiting Guth's remarks on social media. The case prompted the University of Kansas to adopt a draconian policy that prohibits statements by faculty on social media that are "contrary to the best interests of the university," or anything that "impairs discipline by superiors or harmony among coworkers." Some speculate that the policy at the University of Kansas will have a chilling effect on academic freedom of expression beyond Kansas.

In December 2014, Colin Lively, described as a "hair stylist to the rich and famous in New York City and Cleveland," started a thread on Facebook about the police killings of unarmed black men in Ferguson, Missouri, and Staten Island, New York, and a twelve-year-old child in Cleveland.[18] One of the people who responded to Lively's thread was a friend of a friend named Deborah O'Connor, an instructor at Florida State University's business school. O'Connor's comments on the thread included curse words, racial slurs, homophobic insults, derogatory language about the disabled, and denigrating remarks about President Barack Obama and Attorney General Eric Holder. When challenged about her remarks, O'Connor responded: "I teach at a University, you asshole. What do you do?"

Another Facebook friend of Lively's, Susie Sharp, a technology consultant in Cleveland, read the thread and found O'Connor's comments offensive. Sharp was particularly dismayed by O'Connor's attempt to use her institutional affiliation to shield her remarks. "I think university professors should be held to higher standards," she said. Sharp compiled O'Connor's remarks and sent an e-mail to administrators at FSU that read, in part, "It is unfathomable to me that Florida State University would condone or approve of ANY university staff behaving in this manner in private, much less in public. It is horrifying to me to think that this is the kind of person that FSU employs to instruct our youth."[19]

Shortly after the letter to FSU administration, O'Connor submitted her resignation to Caryn Beck-Dudley, the business school's dean, writing, "I sense that 'the path of least resistance' is for me to resign to forestall a litigation, although I must emphasize that I do NOT believe the punishment fits the 'crime.' As a supporter of FSU since 1975, I feel cheated and betrayed but I love FSU and will continue my loyalty to her forever."[20]

In February 2015, the administration at Marquette University in Milwaukee, Wisconsin, took steps to fire a tenured faculty member in political science for a blog post. John McAdams, an associate professor at Marquette, wrote a blog post in November 2014 that was critical of a teaching assistant, Cheryl Abbate. According to McAdams, Abbate shut down a classroom conversation on gay marriage (Abbate supports it) though a student wanted to continue the discussion (the student opposes it). McAdams blogged about the conflict based on a secret complaint made by the disgruntled student.

Abbate asserts that the professor distorted what happened in class that day. Meanwhile, conservative blogs picked up McAdams's version of the story, and Abbate began receiving hate e-mail. As of this writing, Marquette has begun the process of firing McAdams. For his part, McAdams says "he will not go quietly" and that he plans to sue the university for wrongful termination, contending that his blog post should be protected under the provisions of academic freedom.[21]

Easily the most prominent case highlighting the potential risks of academics' social media use is that of Steven G. Salaita. In the summer of 2014, Salaita posted a series of tweets that were critical of Israel's bombing of Gaza. In one, he wrote, "Note how many times Zionists use words like 'savages' and 'animals.' The bombing of #Gaza isn't strategic. It is racist and punitive." After these tweets appeared, pro-Israel students, faculty members, and donors at the University of Illinois at Urbana-Champaign (UIUC) launched a campaign to force the university to rescind its job offer to Salaita, arguing that his comments were anti-Semitic.[22]

Although the campaign involved students, faculty, and donors, there is strong (albeit not conclusive) evidence that the concerns of donors were uppermost on UIUC Chancellor Phyllis Wise's mind when she made her decision to rescind the offer to Salaita. Wise met with major donors before announcing the decision and held internal meetings with her development staff to gauge the potential effect of her decision.[23] In at least one e-mail to the chancellor, someone who identified himself as a major donor ("Having been a multiple 6 figure donor to Illinois over the years") said that he would stop giving to UIUC if Salaita were hired.[24] While there is no definitive evidence that Wise based her decision about Salaita's hire on these issues, her ultimate decision was consistent with the interests of these powerful donors.

Wise responded to pressure about Salaita's appointment by revoking the offer of a faculty position and characterizing his behavior as "uncivil," but stopped short of calling it anti-Semitic. The *Chronicle of Higher Education* included Salaita in their 2014 "Influence List" of "academic newsmakers that made a mark—for better or worse" that year. On that list, the headline described Salaita as a "Twitter Casualty" for joining "a growing list of college instructors whose statements on social media have spawned backlashes that threaten their careers."[25] In a way, the focus on the 140-character social media platform is striking.

There was little about the Salaita-UIUC controversy that was particular to Twitter per se. Salaita could have posted his comments on Facebook, on Tumblr, or on any other platform. Indeed, he has written at length about his criticisms of Israel and support for Palestinians in several academic books. In some ways, focusing on the role of Twitter in this case serves to deflect attention away from the surrounding political issues: namely, the boycott, divestment, and sanction movement directed at Israel that has been growing within American universities and scholarly associations.

Focusing on the role of Twitter in the Salaita case may also distract us from the powerful role that deep-pocketed donors and trustees play in the governance of today's universities and colleges. It seems clear that it was donors' objections to Salaita's appointment that led to the undoing of his hiring—thus making him much more a casualty of the neoliberal restructuring of higher education than a "Twitter Casualty." Yet the Salaita affair has become, for all intents and purposes, a cautionary tale about academics' Twitter use, so it is worthwhile to explore what his case and others like it tell us about academic freedom in a digitally networked age.

The administrative, legislative, and donor reactions to these cases have had a chilling effect on voices of dissent in higher education. These cases raise important questions about the reach of administrators, legislators, and donors in higher education. These groups are preternaturally sensitive about protecting the image of an academic institution, and they may find offense in faculty members' off-brand messaging from their personal social media accounts. Although it is easy to caution the wise public scholar to take stock of the social, institutional, and political context in which they find themselves and act circumspectly, the shifting sand of the landscape of higher education calls for a more vigilant defense of dissent and academic freedom in the digital age.

Dissent and Digital Scholarship

Visibility can invite negative scrutiny from unhappy research subjects or unknown readers who are simply out to pick a fight. It can lead many of us to chafe in the face of public exposure. Many scholars simply do not have the constitution for being in the public eye; their choices need to be respected. After all, many of us became academics because we like ideas, we like to read and write, and to teach—and we appreciate the relative seclusion offered by an academic job. As the philosopher Richard Rorty once put it, "Universities permit one to read books and report what one thinks about them, and get paid for it."[26]

And yet the cloistered ivory tower is going the way of the card catalog. "We can no longer hold a position of splendid isolation," writes

Michael Burawoy. Rather than think of the era that has disappeared as the Golden Age of the University, the sociologist says, "in reality it was a fool's paradise that simply couldn't last."[27] Today, academics live in an era of greater transparency—and increased scrutiny.

Stories of the kinds of negative pushback that can accompany being a public scholar, such as the ones mentioned above, may lead us to try to retreat even further. They may convince us that it's better to write books and have conversations solely with those who appreciate our insights and who respect our specialized knowledge within the academy. Why should anyone bother turning their research into pithy narratives if the risks to their reputation and, sometimes even to their own livelihoods, are so great?

Well, writes Cheryl Blumley, "quite simply because it's too risky not to do so." The journalist and social science editor asserts that "Silo-ing the great work that academics do within the hallowed, inherently exclusive institutions is a disservice to the public and also, to one's own research."[28] Moreover, if we're to develop a collective civic imagination, cultural critic Henry Giroux urges, public intellectuals have a responsibility to unsettle power, trouble consensus, and challenge common sense. "The very notion of being an engaged public intellectual is neither foreign to, nor a violation of, what it means to be an academic scholar, but central to its very definition."[29]

Few of us will ever elicit the kinds of sustained negative publicity of a Goffman or a Salaita or a Grundy. Attacking us isn't worth all the trouble. But whenever we send our research into the world, we become potential targets. Attacks on the few threaten all of us, and challenge our collective right to dissent. The Internet has extended the reach of those who do not like our opinions, amplifying their voices. Those who belong to underrepresented groups must confront the social realities of racism, sexism, and homophobia wherever we go, including online.

"Don't read the comments" is a truism of the Internet, as people so often feel emboldened to say things behind a screen and keyboard that they might not in face-to-face interactions. If you're building an audience online, and if in your embodied self you identify as a woman (whether cis or trans), or a feminist, or queer, or if you are black, Indigenous/Native, Latina/o, or Asian, then there is a much greater likelihood that audiences will harass or verbally attack you (or worse).

Feminist academics Rosie Campbell and Sarah Childs, who are active on Twitter, agree that social media can "be risky for women and for feminists because the anonymity frequently permits hostile interventions." However, it is a risk they choose to take because, they say, "There are also significant opportunities for new voices to disrupt debates, and disseminate [ideas] to those whom we normally don't speak to."[30]

Following her encounter with the far right, Saida Grundy got lots of advice from fellow academics to stay away from social media. Still, she refuses to disengage. For one thing, the kind of attacks Grundy experienced can happen anywhere. "These issues are unavoidable for a person of color who work[s] on issues of race. The idea that if you shut down social media, you will avoid the battles, that is a fallacy," she says. If we allow people to intimidate public scholars, says Grundy, we "wouldn't know a lot of what we do about global warming" or the effectiveness of vaccinations in eliminating disease. When someone who claims to have graduated from the "University of Google"[31] says that they "know more about immunization and vaccines than medical doctors," something's wrong.[32]

Even those who write primarily for scholarly audiences are never entirely immune from criticism, or uncivil discourse, or sharply opposing views. The only sure way for scholars to escape any and all controversy is by doing unremarkable work that contributes little of broad interest, or work that is so inconsequential—or impenetrable—that it's incapable of ruffling anyone's feathers because so few people care about it, or understand it. As should be clear by now, we don't endorse such an approach.

While there are certainly additional risks in being a public scholar, particularly as university policies about academic freedom haven't yet caught up with the realities of social media, the need for dissent remains urgent.[33] While it's impossible to avoid controversy altogether when undertaking public work, it's still important to protect yourself.

Guard Your Privacy, Know Your Rights— and Develop a Thick Skin

"No matter how many times a privileged straight white male technology executive pronounces the death of privacy, privacy is not dead," says danah boyd, who studies the Internet. boyd is referring to the myth, promulgated by people like Google CEO Eric Schmidt, that no one cares about privacy in the digital age, particularly younger people, who've always had the Internet. That's just not true, says boyd. "People of all ages care deeply about privacy. And they care just as much about privacy online as they do offline."[34]

But things are changing. Privacy looks different today. We tend to imagine public and private as a binary pair, a set of polar opposites. It's not so simple anymore, according to boyd. Before the Internet, a face-to-face conversation that you might have in a hallway was private by default, and public through some effort. That hallway conversation would, most likely, end up staying private because no one bothered to share what was said. If the conversation contained some news worth spreading, then that conversation might be made public.

Now, when you engage online in settings like someone's Facebook wall, the conversation is public *by default*, because that's the way the platform is set up. "You actually have to think about making something private," boyd says, "because by default, it is going to be accessible to a much broader audience." This shift requires a different set of calculations, a different set of choices. "You have to choose to limit access rather than assuming that it won't spread very far," boyd explains. "And, needless to say, people make a lot of mistakes learning this."[35]

Guarding one's privacy while maintaining a network of connections is therefore an important, even crucial, skill for the twenty-first-century citizen and public scholar to learn. "Wanting privacy is not about needing something to hide," boyd explains, "it's about wanting to maintain control." boyd developed a series of questions for teens as guidelines for guarding privacy online: What are you trying to achieve? Whom do you think you're talking to? How would you feel if someone else was looking? What if what you said could be misinterpreted? Similar considerations apply to scholars, too.

For example, some scholars are very deliberate about the kinds of personal details they choose to share publicly. While some people may be oversharing "the small, sorry details" through endless status updates, others are going deeper and carving meaning out of the "hard and unforgiving material of a life."[36] Literature professor Michael Bérubé wrote a moving personal essay on his son's Down syndrome, "Life as We Know It: A Father, a Son and Genetic Destiny," which appeared in *Harper's* magazine, and has been widely anthologized. When journalist Melissa Harris-Perry gave birth using in vitro fertilization, she wrote about her trepidation and joy in a piece called "How We Made Our Miracle," which appeared on MSNBC's website. Both Harris-Perry and Bérubé shared stories about their families to make larger points, but took care to insure that the bulk of their personal lives remained private and protected from public view; in Harris-Perry's story we never even learn the name of her daughter.

Knowing your rights is important, too. As of this writing, faculty unions, professional associations, colleges, and universities are all woefully behind in adopting policies that protect scholars who come under attack for their engagement in the public sphere. While your institution may have some resources, you're going to have to look for them. Ask if your college or university has a media office. Find out if your institution has a protocol in place for threats against its faculty. Look into faculty governance, such as the faculty senate, and ask if they have a clear policy in place about social media and public scholarship. Contact your professional association to see if they have any resources for besieged members. And, finally, if you're in a faculty union, find out if they protect academic freedom.[37]

Public scholars also need to develop a pretty thick skin. Lisa Wade says she is able to quickly "dismiss and ignore criticisms that are just obviously stupid. Someone who tells me I should 'suck a dick and die' does not bother me at all, even for a half second," she says, because such comments are meant to do little more than provoke. "You just have to learn to let it go," agrees Tufekci. "You're going to have fans and detractors—sometimes you can learn from detractors—but you have to let it go. If something [someone sends me] looks awful, I just put it in a folder and don't look at it." She saves it as evidence, just in case she needs it in the future. Tufekci also changes the default settings on platforms, adjusting the settings so that she doesn't see or hear troublesome people. And she creates what she calls her own "safe spaces" online, including a Twitter list comprised of other academics that she follows. "It saves me from the main feed but allows me to see the people I want to see," she says.

Creating "safe spaces" online can be an effective way of turning down the volume on disturbing events in the news. If you, like Tufekci, study a subject that routinely involves a lot of human misery, it's important to find ways to step back from that. Developing a thick skin may also include stepping away from social media, closing the laptop, leaving the smart phone at home or turned off, and going for a walk. Or it may mean enlisting the help of a friend to help you sort through vicious comments online or through your inbox. In the early days of the Internet, heated discussions were called "flame wars," and these have a way of raising one's blood pressure. The key to handling the rough-and-tumble of online attacks is finding whatever helps you lower your blood pressure.

After enduring taunts and harassment for her book *Not Gay*, Jane Ward decided to have a little fun with her detractors, and she began to "perform" some of the responses she received. In an invitation to a book talk, she explained:

Come join me as I read from my loved and hated book. Topics covered: brojobs, feminist rage, dicks (the body part and the subjectivity), whiteness, repulsion, love, gays vs. queers, gaysplaining, and "stupid whores who write books about subjects they have no business writing about" (e.g., me). In addition to the conventional reading, I will be performatively engaging with email I have received from strangers commenting on the book—hate mail, lust mail, and mail truly resisting categorization.[38]

Having a thick skin may entail talking back to your critics. It may also, at times, mean avoiding unnecessary conflicts. "It's easy to become defensive and write something one later regrets, but the fact is snotty exchanges can be Googled," cautions Lester Andrist, who helps run the *Sociological Cinema*. Managing a multiuser platform is a slightly different proposition than being attacked as an individual, but a lot of the same principles apply.

"It's important to know when it is not worth responding to a comment, when it is important to delete a comment, or when it is necessary to ban a user," he says. Whenever he's responding to a cantankerous individual, Andrist says he tries to stay professional, respectful, and "when you've made a mistake, it's almost always a good idea to just apologize." Humility is a good quality to have if you're going to be a public scholar—though it's no match for bombs and guns.

Real Harm, Everyday Life

In modern life we must parse real threats from the exaggerated worries promulgated on cable news channels. Though we fear violence in schools, writes Barry Glassner, we're about three times more likely to be struck by lightning.[39] But harm is not always an illusory threat.

When Anita Sarkeesian was invited to give a talk at Utah State University about her work on the stereotypes of women in video games, the university received a credible bomb threat. She planned to go ahead with her talk; bomb threats against her have become routine. Then, the day before her talk was scheduled, administrators at Utah State received an e-mail that warned, "This will be the deadliest school shooting in American history, and I'm giving you a chance to stop it." The e-mail bore the moniker Marc Lépine, the name of a man who killed fourteen women in a mass shooting at an engineering school in Montreal in 1989; following the massacre, he committed suicide.

Under Utah law, campus police could not prevent people with weapons from entering her talk. That's when she decided to cancel it.[40] The attacks on Sarkeesian are part of a larger campaign to discredit or intimidate critics of the male-dominated gaming industry and its culture who are associated with the Twitter hashtag #GamerGate. The hashtag has become a shorthand among those who criticize articles or opinion columns on gamer sites that are sympathetic to feminist critics of the industry.[41]

Activism can at times be life threatening. Bonnie Jouhari is a former social worker who helped people file housing discrimination complaints in the Reading, Pennsylvania, area. Jouhari is white and the mother of a biracial child. Her work on housing justice and her identity, and that of her child, apparently enraged a local white supremacist. In March of 1998, a white supremacist website began posting pictures online of Jouhari's workplace, which he had altered so that it appeared to be exploding amid computer-animated video flames. Jouhari and her daughter began receiving threatening telephone calls and notes on her car. Jouhari was forced to move first to another town in Pennsylvania, then to Seattle, and eventually to an undisclosed location, in order to get away from the ongoing threat to her and her child.[42]

The attacks endured by Sarkeesian and Jouhari could happen to anyone that crossed the wrong #GamerGate dude or the wrong white supremacist. The fact that most of this abuse happens to women, who are almost always targeted by men, leads some to suggest that online attacks could be considered hate crimes.[43] That's why some feminists are leading efforts to reform social media platforms.[44]

When a Change.org petition with more than two hundred thousand signatures failed to prompt Facebook to remove rape "humor" groups, three women took action. They wrote an open letter to Facebook and partnered with a coalition of women's and human rights groups to ask members to write to advertisers to question why their ads were appearing against this kind of user-generated content. Together, the coalition of activists sent five thousand e-mails to Facebook's advertisers and generated sixty thousand tweets.

Within a week, Facebook acquiesced and changed its definition of hate speech and said in a statement, "defense of freedom of expression should never be interpreted as a license to bully, harass, abuse or threaten violence." Jaclyn Friedman, one of the organizers said, "I think for so long people thought: 'This is so awful, what can you do?' And I'm hoping that this success story will send a message saying well: 'You can keep trying things until you find something that works.'"[45] This sort of change is what's needed for public scholars, especially those with dissenting views, to thrive.

Conclusion

Many scholars wish to contribute to the public good in some way. But when we go public, we run the risk of our work being misunderstood or misinterpreted; there may be angry subjects who speak back in ways that are difficult to reconcile with our findings and our hopes. We also risk failing in public: when we work out our ideas in public, our mistakes can become public, too.

Being a public scholar doesn't mean sharing everything. Understanding that *public* is now the default setting on most social media platforms, we must actively maintain some control over our lives. Sometimes that means learning to ignore attacks, or filter out the noise when it becomes too loud, frequent, or personal. While we learn new ways of managing public and private information, we also need to know our rights within a given geographic location, institutional setting, and professional affiliation. One thing is certain:

we can no longer expect to toil in a sequestered ivory tower where only a tiny handful of other academics will see our work. At the same time, if we labor in higher education today and ignore the public, we do so at our own peril. It is precisely in these precarious times that loud, vocal, unapologetic dissent from public scholars is more crucial than ever.

... 7 ...

Making It Count, Making a Difference

In the classic 1946 Frank Capra film *It's a Wonderful Life*, Jimmy Stewart's character, George Bailey, on the verge of suicide, is given the gift of seeing what the world would have been like without him in it. A guardian angel, Clarence, replays key events in his life in Bedford Falls, New York, and then runs the reel of what would have unfolded if he hadn't been there. "Your brother died, George, because you weren't there to save him when he fell through the ice," Clarence explains. In another scene, he reveals that there isn't even a "Bedford Falls." The town becomes "Pottersville," overrun by the evil banking overlord Mr. Potter (played by Lionel Barrymore), all because George Bailey wasn't there to stop him. As he sees more and more of this alternative reality without him in it, George Bailey begs, "I want to live again." His wish is granted. Cue the happy ending.

In many ways *It's a Wonderful Life* is about the importance of making an impact. Imagine if George Bailey had been an academic. Would Clarence-the-guardian-angel tell George Bailey, "Life is worth living, George, look how many articles you've published, and how many citations you have. Look at how high your H-index is!" No. There are many things in life more important, and more meaningful, than that. In fact, the desire to create meaningful lives is what drew most of us to academic work to begin with.

Historically, universities have been places where we participate in the (relatively) free exchange of ideas. Inside and outside of these institutions, intellectuals have played the role of social critic, holding up a mirror to society so that we can see ourselves more clearly. Even today, in a world where commercial imperatives shape nearly every aspect of life, higher education continues to be a sphere that nourishes the civic imagination. Many of us embark on academic careers for this reason, and with the vague notion that we want to make a difference and have an impact on the world.

Unfortunately, the graduate school experience—a long, difficult process whose goal is to make us into producers of knowledge and workers in the knowledge factory—often leads us to shed our loftier aspirations. Discussions about the impact of our work, if they happen at all, tend to be framed in the narrowest of terms, such as how many citations stack up after one of your articles is published. In order to keep our jobs and advance in them, we must abide by the rules of academia, cultivate professional personae, and justify the value of our work.

The pursuit of individual self-interest and simultaneous cultivation of the spirit of engaged inquiry characterizes the life of the academic today. That means making an impact also requires us, to a great extent, to be able to measure that impact so that we can justify our work to hiring and promotion committees, academic administrators, and even sometimes to the public officials who allocate funds for the institutions in which we work. Today, it's not enough to cultivate the life of the mind: we must also demonstrate our social, political, and even economic utility. As public scholars, how do we take the work we do and make it "count" in ways that are legible to academic institutions? How can those of us who are doing unconventional work make it count in conventional ways? And, how, finally, can we make a difference?

Beyond Counting Citations

For most of the twentieth century, most disciplines measured scholarly impact by counting the number of times someone had published in peer-reviewed journals and the number of citations of those publications in other peer-reviewed journals. The Social Sciences Citation Index (SSCI) compiles and indexes these citations across fifty disciplines and several thousand journals. The SSCI is a commercial enterprise; the volume is sold to college and university libraries for a hefty fee so that college deans and presidents can use it to measure faculty research productivity. The SSCI combs the journals for citations, and then lists them after an individual scholar's name. So, if we were to look up "Daniels, Jessie" in the SSCI, we would find, underneath the name, a list of all the places where her peer-reviewed articles have been cited in other peer-reviewed journals.

In the days of analog-only measurement, tenure and promotion committees would send grad student assistants to the library with an actual ruler in order to measure the number of inches a prospective candidate had in the SSCI. Sometimes a ruler is just a ruler—but this strategy suggests an obsession with size, measured in inches. In institutions where one's job relies on succeeding in relation to such measures, this is no laughing matter.

While these traditional, rather crude, measures may still prevail at some colleges and universities, there are additional, new ways to measure impact. Alternative metrics, known as "altmetrics," are also now widely discussed as a possible way of measuring influence, though they are not yet uniformly used. There are a number of ways to measure the impact of publicly engaged scholarship and make those measures understandable to hiring, tenure, and promotion committees. A growing number of PhD-holders are also turning to alternative academic careers that combine public scholarship with life outside the tenure track—sometimes referred to as "alt-ac" careers.

Whether we move between traditional and alt-ac tracts, are resolutely committed to pursuing a tenure-track job, or are holding a tenured position now, we all have reasons to want to measure our impact and tell a story about it that makes sense to other people, particularly to those people who make decisions about hiring, tenure, and such things. Here are a few principles to help guide you in figuring out how to measure your impact as a public scholar in a way that is meaningful for you and, perhaps, comprehensible to your institution.

Principle #1: Know What Counts at Your Institution

"Will this count for tenure?" is a question that plagues academics on the tenure track. Many people suggest that everything you do in those early career days should be an activity that "counts" toward tenure, either directly (like getting a peer-reviewed publication out the door) or indirectly (like attending a conference where you might cultivate peer reviewers for the eventual tenure file). It is important to pay attention to what your institution will recognize as part of your portfolio, especially at the end of the first-year, third-year, and sixth-year tenure reviews (or whatever your institution marks as the most important benchmarks).

Academic institutions, and their standards for tenure, vary widely across the United States. As you might expect, there are also wide variations in standards for tenure and promotion at institutions outside the United States. Traditionally, in order to receive tenure one must establish a "national reputation" as a scholar; for promotion to full professor, one must demonstrate a reputation that is sufficiently "international." It is the task of peer reviewers, other scholars in one's field, to assess whether an individual scholar has achieved such a reputation. In addition to soliciting the review of peers (typically in the sixth or seventh year), there are many other internal reviews and quantifiable measures.

Even before you begin, find out whether your department looks more favorably upon writing books or publishing journal articles. If publishing a book-length manuscript is the key measure of your scholarly accomplishment, a university press that sends manuscripts out for peer review is the generally accepted standard for establishing a reputation as a scholar with a national reputation. But if your department expects you to publish articles in peer-reviewed journals, find out how many articles you're expected to produce before going up for tenure. Ideally, your institution will have this written down somewhere in tenure and promotion guidelines, but if not, there are other ways to find out. Talk to people who make these decisions and ask them. Find people who have recently, and successfully, gone through the tenure process and ask them how many articles they published; and find people at comparable institutions and ask them the same.

You should also find out what kind of journals your department expects you to publish in. This may seem obvious, but if you are doing work that's interdisciplinary and could be published in different kinds of journals, it's important to find out if some of these journals "count" more than others. Some institutions consider something called "journal impact factor" (JIF). Most publishers list their journals' impact factor somewhere on their websites. Traditionally the higher the JIF, the more prestigious the journal.

For example, let's look at two journals that Jessie has published articles in. The *American Journal of Public Health* (*AJPH*) has a journal impact factor of 3.566, while *Gender & Society* (*G&S*) has a JIF of 1.339. In the crudest use of this measure, a committee would give the publication in *AJPH* more weight than the publication in *G&S*. However, a department that doesn't reward interdisciplinary work might not "count" either publication if it were not among the top journals in the field. Some committees will only count articles in the same field as the department in which the candidate holds a position. And, of course, many departments expect a mix of a book and several articles in order to demonstrate scholarly success. Know what your institution expects.

Some departments and institutions, such as Harvard University, MIT, and Virginia Commonwealth University, require faculty work to be available open access, either by posting online yourself (self-archiving) or by publishing it in an open-access journal.[1] Again, it's important to know what the policies are at your institution because they are not uniform.

Many institutions will view one's social media presence as a distraction from the "real" work of being an academic who would be better served spending that time writing articles for peer-reviewed journals, or books for academic presses. "Until you get tenure, social media is extra," religious studies and Africana studies professor Anthea Butler advises.[2] It's hard to argue with this advice, especially if you work at a place that abides by traditional measures of scholarly accomplishment. As sociologist Barry Wellman quips, "I've never known someone to get tenure for a blog post."[3] While this may be sage—and safe—advice at this point, your social media presence as an academic may help you in ways that *do* count toward tenure at your institution.

Literature scholar Patricia Matthew writes about the "calculated risk" she took when she began blogging and engaging on Twitter as an untenured assistant professor. She started an academic blog about her scholarly work on race and tenure in the humanities. After consulting with a few people at her institution, she added a section to her curriculum vitae called "Public Writing," listing her scholarly blog, along with the sites' statistics demonstrating reach and the most relevant cross-postings. Still, Matthew has this cautionary advice for pre-tenure folks:

> I want to be very clear here: I don't believe that blogging of the kind
> that I do will prop up a weak file or distract from the absence of
> peer-reviewed publications that are still the gold standard in my

discipline. In fact, I can easily imagine a scenario where a skeptical personnel committee or administrator might see blogging as a distraction from the "real" work of traditional, peer-reviewed scholarship.[4]

Unexpectedly, Matthew says, her blogging led to opportunities for doing more traditional academic work, like publishing in peer-reviewed journals, conference presentations, invited talks, and service in her field beyond her department. Because she had a scholarly blog and an active Twitter presence, she began to get invitations she might not have received otherwise. Editors at two prestigious journals invited her to review the latest books in the field; organizers invited her to participate in a panel at a conference that included some of the heavy hitters in the field; and now she is working with those same people to turn that panel discussion into a publication for the organization's top journal. Matthew's experience illustrates how academics are using social media to help them advance within the academy. When people can find your work online and read it, it can generate invitations to contribute work to more traditionally recognized academic endeavors.

The takeaway here is that publishing, teaching, and service—primarily publishing—continue to determine hiring and promotion decisions in the academy. "You have to do the peer-reviewed publishing just as much," advises Zeynep Tufekci, who became a very visible public scholar while an assistant professor. "I have journal articles, a book with university press, and an NSF grant." So, when the *New York Times* asked her to become a regular contributor, she checked with her dean (she was going up for tenure) and with her book publisher (her book would be late). "They were both very supportive," she says, adding that her institution values public engagement. The book publisher knew that her platform at the *Times* would eventually help sell books, even if the manuscript came later.

People are using their online presence to increase their opportunities for doing academic work that will be evaluated favorably in such decisions. Some institutions are beginning to recognize things like a "Public Writing" section on a junior academic's CV as part of a portfolio that demonstrates a national reputation—though, again, not all do. This shift is happening slowly, incrementally, and unevenly, so it's crucial to know your institution's expectations for demonstrating your achievements.

Principle #2: Make your Research Easy to Find

We've encouraged this in different ways before here, but it bears repeating: if you have an interest in being a public scholar, you should make your research easy to find through search engines. People are most likely to find your research using a search engine. It's also useful for the people who are likely to do a tenure review, who are often doing a dozen or so a year, to be able to quickly find your research online. There are a number of fairly straightforward ways to do this.

When you give your next conference presentation or journal article a title, consider whether it accurately conveys the main point of the article. Some academics are too clever by half when they name their papers with elaborate, obscure, and long titles that hide rather than reveal their emphasis. Almost all journals require that you submit four or five keywords to go along with your paper. When you choose keywords, consider whether they are also in the title. They don't need to match exactly, but they should bear some relationship to each other. The title and the keywords are part of what librarians and information scientists call "metadata"—what makes your research findable in the vast sea of information in digital archives.

Post your paper, or at least a version of it, on your institutional repository (IR). Institutional repositories are "digital collections of the outputs created within a university or research institution," basically a website for all the papers, articles, books, digital projects, and other "outputs" that people have created at one institution.[5] An IR is both a way for universities to showcase the work happening in their institutions and a place for faculty and graduate students to make their work available. As of this writing, over six hundred colleges and universities in the United States have an institutional repository, and many more exist outside the United States. If you want to find out if your institution has an IR, you can check the list at OpenDOAR (http://www.opendoar.org/countrylist.php). The requirement we mentioned earlier, that some universities have to make your work available open access, often appears in conjunction with an IR. The goal is to circulate research outside the university, where it might be useful to people, or as Harvard Provost Steven Hyman says, "where so much of our research is of global significance, we have an essential responsibility to distribute the fruits of our scholarship as widely as possible."[6]

There are also repositories for specific subject areas. So, for example, if you are doing public policy research, you may want to post your research at the Policy Archive (http://www.policyarchive.org/). If you are in folklore studies, there is a specific archive for that field (https://scholarworks.iu.edu/dspace/handle/2022/3849). And, for the social sciences more broadly, there is the Social Sciences Research Network (http://www.ssrn.com/en/). If you publish in medicine or public health and related fields, PubMed searches the metadata and compiles publications (some full text, others only in abstract). The Open Access Directory has a list of all the subject and disciplinary repositories (http://oad.simmons.edu/oadwiki/Disciplinary _repositories), and you can check each of them for instructions on how to post your work there. Most journals have a "no prior publication" requirement for work submitted to them, but making your work available through a repository is not the same thing as publishing it. In fact, the subject repository SSRN addresses this directly in their frequently asked questions section:

> We are unaware of any journals that consider SSRN's eLibrary or the email abstract eJournals to be "prior publication" since our services are basically an aggregation of working papers and not a refereeing process. If an author requests it, we will immediately remove their

paper from the SSRN eLibrary. (http://www.ssrn.com/en/index.cfm/ssrn-faq/#no_paper_sub)

You don't need to post your work in *all* the repositories. Just pick one that makes the most sense for you and your work. If you have a tenure-track or tenured position at an institution with a repository, then it may make sense to use that one. Some institutions require it or strongly encourage it, though this is less common in the United States than it is in other countries. You may also want to use the IR at your institution while you're a graduate student, but as you go on to a tenure-track job, you may then decide to move your work to another repository. You can also make you work easy to find by posting it on your personal website, which we talked about at length in chapter 3. This is an excellent alternative if you don't have access to an institutional repository or if you are a mobile academic.

Many scholars worry about the rules of copyright when it comes to making their work easy to find on the web. To be sure, the current landscape of copyright and academic journals is potentially very confusing, and it's quickly changing, which makes it even harder. However, a simple guideline to help make things easier is that most journals have copyright rules that allow what's known as the "pre-print" version—before the final formatting and the logo of the journal is added—to be made publicly available.[7] Increasingly, many journals also allow the final, formatted version of the paper to be posted online after an embargo period of a year to two. The copyright rules vary with each journal publisher, so pay attention to what the rules are for the journals in your field. There is a very handy resource for figuring this out, called SherpaRomeo (http://www.sherpa.ac.uk/romeo/), which is an all-volunteer project run by librarians who compile publisher copyright policies for scholars worldwide.

You can post your work online, legally, and not run afoul of copyright laws, but not every version of every paper you publish can or should be posted everywhere. Scholars need to be savvy about copyright and authors' rights in the digital age. It's a complicated field, and it can seem confusing at first. In one particularly vexing incident in the battle over authors' rights, the commercial publisher Elsevier demanded that authors remove publications they had posted to Academia.edu (also a commercial platform). In this case, individual researchers and Academia.edu pushed back against Elsevier, but such incidents can make posting your work online seem like a minefield—particularly after you've worked so hard to get a paper published.

As a general guideline, it's almost always the case that journals allow you to post what's called a preprint version of an article once the article has been published. Other journals allow you to post the formatted PDF version of the paper, but only after a waiting period, or "embargo." So, for instance, when you have a paper accepted for publication, you might post a preprint version on your website or IR, then when the embargo period ends, replace that with the formatted version with the logo of the journal. Even if the journal is not open access, this practice of "self-archiving" can make your research findable by search engines. When in doubt, check the SherpaRomeo tool for the rules of the journal you're publishing in. And, if you want help some hands-on help with this, you might check with your campus library. There are often librarians with expertise in open access, authors' rights, and journal copyright that can help guide you through this terrain.

For books, copyright generally resides with the publishing house. But many authors, including academic ones, are now beginning to negotiate with book publishers for at least some rights to their books. For example, Yale University Press granted legal scholar Julia E. Cohen (*Configuring the Networked Self*) and social media scholar danah boyd (*It's Complicated*) the right to post free PDFs of their books online while simultaneously selling books in the standard formats.[8] Other book publishers allow individual chapters to be released free and online alongside more traditional sales options. And some publishers allow time-limited, open-access versions of the book (or parts of it) to be made available for events or open, online courses.[9] There is such wide variation in these policies, and the rules are changing so quickly, that the author has to be willing to ask for the rights or they will, by default, reside with the publisher forever. If you'd like to learn more about your rights as a book author, the nonprofit Authors Alliance (http://www.authorsalliance.org/) is working with writers to help them better understand and manage key legal, technological, and institutional aspects of what the rights of book authorship are in the digital age.

Again, check with the librarians at your institution and find one who is familiar with copyright and open access for further guidance. In the case of books, the general guideline is that by default, the rights to your work will always and in perpetuity go to the publisher, who stands to profit from your work. It's up to you, the author of those words, to try (at the very least) to understand what those terms are and, if you can, negotiate for copyright terms that allow you to make your work easily accessible to the widest possible audience.

But . . . What If Someone Steals My Ideas?

A frequent objection to posting work online is the fear that "someone will steal my ideas." Theft is, unfortunately, not new to the academy. For many years, certain forms of theft and plunder were so common as to be institutionalized. Norval Glenn, a sociologist, tells a story about being listed as the second author on the book based on his dissertation research. The first author? The dissertation supervisor, of course.

While this kind of routinized theft may happen less frequently now, some scholars worry that making their research easy to find online will also make it easier to steal. Yet, evidence to support the claim that work posted online gets stolen is hard to find. Emily VanBuren, a graduate student in history, wrote a thoughtful piece for *Grad Hacker* pondering whether or not she should launch a blog about her PhD research. While most of the comments she received were encouraging, someone with the user name "AroundaLongTime" wrote the following: "Please keep a diary for yourself, not a blog. Your ideas will be stolen. Believe me, while waiting for articles to appear, someone else published the same."[10] VanBuren wrote back and pressed for details, but AroundaLongTime was no longer around and didn't reply with specifics about their experience. As is frequently the case, there's lots of concern, but little evidence that anything had actually happened.

Posting your work online may in fact be the very best way to "protect your ideas" from being stolen. It may also be one of the most effective ways to build your audience. Take, for example, the novelist Paulo Coelho, who "pirates" his own work. That is, he takes entire books and posts them online for free and without his publisher's permission. In 2000, Coelho found a pirated Russian translation of his book *The Alchemist* that was selling about one thousand copies a year in Russia. After he put the pirated (free) version online in 2001, the book *sold* ten thousand copies. The next year it sold over one hundred thousand, even though the publisher had not done any promotion in Russia. People downloaded it, started reading it, liked it, and then bought the version the publisher was selling. By 2008, there were over 10 million copies of the book sold in Russia.[11] Most scholars who are considering whether or not to post their work online have a considerably smaller potential audience than Coelho. Yet his experience speaks to the changing nature of copyright, property, and publishing in the digital age. What Coelho's example suggests is that it may be harder than ever to "protect" work online, and it may counterproductive if you want to reach the widest possible readership.

Hiding research until publication in a peer-reviewed journal or academic book suggests a fundamental misunderstanding of how the research process often works. In the social sciences, there is never a eureka moment of discovery in some hidden-away research lab that is then revealed, *et voilà*, upon publication in a peer-reviewed journal. There is instead a slow, sometimes years-long accretion of knowledge and growing expertise that is developed through exchange with others who are thinking about the same topic or set of ideas.

Traditionally, academics have engaged in this exchange of ideas through face-to-face conferences with other academics, and through correspondence: at one time through letters, and more recently through e-mails. The digital turn in academia has moved such conversations out of those cloistered settings into a more or less public domain that opens scholarly conversations up to a wider set of peers and interested listeners. Given the challenging academic job market and the general fear about "stranger danger" on the Internet, it makes sense that there might be anxiety about having one's academic work stolen online. Rest assured, though, that the digital technologies that make it easy to share work online also make it fairly simple to track when, where, and how your research is being used. And in many respects, making your work easy to find establishes you as one of the experts in your field even before you get to the peer-reviewed publication stage.

Unscrupulous advisors and other academics will take someone else's ideas and use them without attribution and claim them as their own, original thoughts at times. Shameful. And true. In the digital era, there are a host of new concerns about plagiarism and stealing ideas, and frequently, these kinds of stories involve academics lifting ideas from community activists under the guise of "research" but without benefit of institutional review or attribution.

The ease of copy-and-paste technology makes it alarmingly easy to commit plagiarism. Academics are not immune from doing this, and they may even be particularly susceptible to doing it. What else but a copy-and-paste error could explain the recent kerfuffle involving Slovenian philosopher Slavoj Žižek, who was accused of plagiarizing a white supremacist online magazine for a piece he wrote for the academic journal *Critical Inquiry*?[12] Unintentional plagiarism and theft are surely near the top of the list of hazards for scholars in the digital era, and there's certainly no more unpleasant way of "going public" than being accused of plagiarism.

The Internet is based on a "sharing" or gift economy, says legal scholar and digital media expert Yochai Benkler.[13] Sociologist Deborah Lupton extends this metaphor to encompass what she calls "networked scholarship." Academic blogging is a medium that often serves the purpose of sharing information and providing advice as part of a gift economy of producing material to share freely with others, she writes. In other words, scholarship and knowledge that circulate in this way are social goods that enhance participatory democracy—not marketable commodities.[14] Legal dilemmas surrounding ownership of intellectual property in digital environments—who owns what ideas—abound, and remain unresolved. As in so many arenas, the law lags considerably behind the technology here.[15]

Since academic advancement revolves around making reputations and crediting ideas, scholars are less inclined to share work if they're not acknowledged for it. That's where Creative Commons (CC) comes in. CC is a set of copyright licenses and tools that give people simple, standardized ways to grant copyright permissions to copy, edit, remix, distribute, and build upon work that's already been done while at the same time making sure to give credit, or "attribution," to the person who created the work. When Jessie published some work on "cloaked websites," she initially thought about copyrighting the term.[16] Then she realized that this was silly because she didn't want to "protect" the idea or make money from it. She wanted the idea to circulate and for people to give her credit for it. Current copyright law does little to protect the work of individual academics and a lot to protect large, moneyed interests, including those in higher ed. CC licensing, developed by Harvard professor Larry Lessig, is a more realistic way of thinking about intellectual property in the digital age. There are a number of different kinds of CC licensing, but the three that are probably most relevant for scholars are "attribution" (giving credit), "non-commercial" (you can't profit from my ideas), and "share-alike" (share your work in the same way).[17] Shifting from analog-based copyright laws designed to "protect ideas" to a Creative Commons model enables scholars to build their reputations and get credit for their ideas at a time when both of these circulate through digital networks.

Principle #3: Track Your Research

There are many tools that can automatically track your research. Earlier, we mentioned alternative metrics, or "altmetrics," a term that emerged in 2010 to describe a range of new methods for analyzing and informing scholarship using the social web.[18] The discussion of altmetrics grew out of the recognition that since no one can read everything, filters can help sort through what's relevant and important for us to read. The kinds of filters we use are changing because the digital technologies we use are changing. Research data expert Heather Piwowar gives a succinct explanation: "Altmetrics give a fuller picture of how research products have influenced conversation, thought and behavior."[19] Altmetrics may expand our view of what impact looks like and how we measure it. As scholarship is created, discussed, and disseminated in an increasingly wide variety of ways, altmetrics offers a range of new measures beyond the journal impact factor, offering an array of tools that keep track of these alternative measures.

Institutional repositories often have some sort of measurement built into the interface, such as number of downloads per month. Academic networks such as SSRN, Academia.edu, or ResearchGate also have measurement built into the platform, including proportional statistics such as "Your paper is in the top 1 percent" in terms of number of downloads in a period of time. Increasingly, academic journals—like many news organizations—generate lists of the most frequently read articles, although the actual numbers of readers, or downloads, for journals or individual articles remain closely guarded industry secrets.

At this point, altmetrics like "number of downloads" say something about *reach*, or the size of an audience, which can be one way to gauge impact. For instance, as we mentioned, the *Sociological Images* blog has a reach of some 2 million readers, an altmetric that suggests a very wide reach, indeed. Further assessment of the quality of that reach requires an evaluative judgment by people qualified to make such judgments. So, when her professional association awarded Lisa Wade the Teaching Sociology Award, a committee of her peers evaluated the impact of her work at the blog and decided that it was changing the way that people teach sociology.

Altmetrics like "Your article is most downloaded" or "Top 1 percent" mainly serve the interest of the publications or the platforms. It's not clear if any tenure or promotion committees are considering these kinds of measures in their decisions. However, altmetrics may help boost more conventional measures of scholarly impact. There's growing evidence to suggest that articles shared on social media are more widely cited in traditional, peer-reviewed literature. One study found that academic papers mentioned on Twitter are more downloaded and cited than papers that are not mentioned there.[20]

Another tool that keeps track of your research for you with a range of different measures is Google Scholar. When you set up a profile on Google Scholar, the platform automatically searches the web for your published, peer-reviewed research. It also looks for citations of your research, much like the analog Social Sciences Citation Index, and combines those into a calculation of an "H-index," which gauges the impact of the work of an individual scholar through an algorithm that includes both productivity (how many articles or books you've published) and how frequently these are cited. On the Google Scholar profile page, you can also find a trend analysis of your work over time. Some scholars include these kinds of measures on an additional page on their CV, much like Patricia Matthew accomplished with her "Public Writing" section. It's not clear whether these types of measures are being utilized by review committees within higher education, so the advice running throughout these principles remains the same: check with your institution about what's accepted practice.

Altmetrics may not be in the same universe as your institution's promotion infrastructure, but this kind of data can be useful in other career-advancing ways. For instance, grant funders and book publishers are often eager to see these kinds of measures of an individual scholar's platform. So, even if your institution doesn't take altmetrics into account for tenure and promotion, you may want to track your research anyway.

Principle #4: Familiarize Yourself with Different Types of Measurement

There are lots of ways to have an impact as a public scholar, and just as many ways to measure that impact. Your specific discipline, area of specialization, and method of study may each have very different types of measurement to demonstrate impact. If you are moving into writing grants to support your research, it's very likely that you'll be asked to come up with your own metrics for determining how successful your funded research has been.

There is a lot more discussion about how to measure research impact in the United Kingdom, in large part because there is a funding structure for higher education there that relies heavily on something called the REF, or Research Excellence Framework. Science policy expert James Wilsdon and a group of colleagues spent fifteen months gathering evidence about the "rising tide" of research measurement in Britain. They propose a framework for what they call "responsible metrics," including one they call "Diversity," by which they mean accounting for variation by field and using a range of indicators to reflect and support a plurality of research and researcher career paths across the system.[21]

In the United States, some institutions, such as the University of Minnesota, are developing a set of public engagement metrics for their faculty. These include measures such as "Evidence of application of research findings by communities" and "Evidence of the contribution of public engagement to student learning." A few scholars and activists have proposed using "transformational" metrics, expanding beyond more traditional "transactional" measures, as a way to build, scale, and support social movements. Transactional metrics include quantitative measures like changing public policy or recruiting participants at a protest or action. Transformational metrics can resemble collaboration or establishing a partnership, something that leads to greater change down the line. The intention behind transformational metrics is to be able to consider impact in ways that are difficult, perhaps impossible, to quantify, but are nevertheless significant.[22] In our work as academics, we tend to think about these kinds of transformational considerations in relation to teaching.

We haven't talked a lot about teaching in this book, one of the primary ways that many academics impact the world, and one of the areas where you need to know how to measure your impact. There are quantitative measures of teaching in place at most colleges and universities. You should become familiar with what these are and how they work at your institution. The more qualitative and potentially long lasting impact of teaching is more difficult to measure. How do we really know if our teaching makes a difference? Humanities scholar Douglas Howard considers the unfinished feeling of so much teaching in general:

> Did Jim, who talked about becoming a therapist, go on to graduate school in psychology? Did Jessica, who argued so passionately in class against the death penalty, make it as a lawyer? We fill in the blanks about them based upon what we know (or think we know), and tell ourselves that their stories ended the way that we hoped. Teaching, in this regard, is the great open-ended narrative, the romantic fragment, the perpetually unfinished symphony.[23]

The fact is we almost never know if a course we taught—or a book we wrote, or an article we labored over—has any impact on anyone else. Media design professor Mark McGuire writes thoughtfully about the difficulty of rating transformational experiences specifically in the context of massive, open, online courses, known as MOOCs:

We rate hotels, music, live performances, movies, etc., so that others are able to make an informed decision about how to best invest their time and money. Rating and reviewing MOOCs seems like a sensible thing to do for similar reasons, and it would not be surprising to see such a practice develop. However, unlike a hotel or restaurant franchise, a living, changing, organic learning experience cannot be packaged, replicated, and sold to consumers who are looking for a satisfying (and predictable) product or service. It can't offer the same experience to the same person twice, and one person's experience may not be a good indicator of the experience another person will have. A transformational learning experience is like a good potluck dinner party—you might have had the time of your life, but it can never be repeated.[24]

We like the dinner party metaphor for teaching much better than the "unfinished symphony," perhaps because both of us are much more likely to attempt a dinner party than a symphony. There is a kind of alchemy in teaching, and in good dinner parties, that makes it easy to assemble the same people, elements, and conditions but difficult to replicate the magic when it happens. The challenge you face early in your career is somehow demonstrating the success of that alchemy, and that brings us back to narrative.

Principle #5: Craft a Narrative about Your Work

In this book we've talked a lot about the importance of storytelling and telling the story of your research. But if you're toiling in the groves of academe, you'll also need to learn to craft a narrative about your career. At some point in the dissertation process, someone probably told you that you need an "elevator pitch" about your research. In reality, since we all meet other people who ask the perennial "so tell me about your work" question, it's good to have a short, concise description of your work for a nonspecialist audience. Once you've got your super-short answer to that question, then you'll need several slightly longer versions of it. Think of it as the 25-word version, then the 50- and 150-word versions of the "story of your work."

In the tenure and promotion process, your audience is made up of those people who decide such matters within your institution. Typically the tenure process starts with a department chair, then goes to a dean of a division, say within arts and sciences, then to some kind of school-wide body (such as a tenure committee), then to a provost and the president of the school, and finally to the board of trustees. Get to know as many of these people as you can. In some ways, the "service" you do (typically the third leg of the three-legged tenure stool), like serving on university-wide committees, is an opportunity to get to know the people who make decisions at your university. As you get to know them, you will learn how they think and talk about scholarship in general. From there, you can learn to craft a narrative with them as an audience in mind.

Death by Metrics?

Just because you can measure something doesn't mean it's important. In fact, the rise of metrics may indicate the demise of the public university and the spirit of free exchange of ideas, according to some critics. The critique of what some call "audit culture" is particularly sharp in Britain, as you might expect, given the emphasis on assessment there.

John Holmwood, a UK sociologist, sees the rush to metrics as emblematic of the neoliberal university, and not coincidentally, as deadly for the social sciences in particular. Holmwood details how disciplines map onto metric performance measured in H-indexes. In such measures, science, technology, engineering, and math fields perform "better" than the social sciences and humanities. Holmwood argues that in the move to corporatize universities and turn them into commercial entities, metric data is a key part of the process. This impacts faculty performance and the student experience. Thus, as Britain has moved to a centralized university application system for all students, it collects metric data on the student experience (in measures such as student satisfaction, graduate employment levels, and income six months after graduation), which it uses in administrative review of each undergraduate degree program. Critics say that this turns students into customers and facilitates an approach to higher education that is rooted in "informed consumer choice" rather than in learners and citizens.[25]

The rise of metrics may also contribute to work speedup and the demise of the university as an idyll where one can "read books, report what one thinks about them, and get paid for it," says UK sociologist Mark Carrigan. Academic work within UK higher education is today potentially subject to more than one hundred different metrics. Instituted in the context of austerity-driven budget cuts, such measures have transformed the life of contemporary academics from a slow-paced contemplative one that pays us to "read books and report what one thinks of them," to that of the accelerated academy, where one must always do more in order to achieve "research excellence."[26] One tragic casualty of these changes was Stefan Grimm, a well-regarded scholar in toxicology in London, who committed suicide after being threatened with losing his job when he was unable to secure sufficient research funding. Interestingly, Carrigan sees the rise of social media as a partial corrective to university restructuring: it offers faculty creative outlets that allow the imagination to thrive. Since it still exists outside of the prevailing systems of audit culture today, the fact that social media doesn't "count" toward tenure is part of what makes it appealing, he says.

An "Upworthy" Academy?

The digital turn challenges those who are steeped in legacy traditions of academia. The suggestion that measures of scholarly impact might change raises concerns that the "popular" will prevail, undermining high quality research. We might call this the "upworthy" problem. If you've ever seen the website Upworthy.com, or been lured into clicking on something there, there's a kind of relentless cheeriness and warm, touchy-feely-ness to it. People who want to endorse content on the website indicate that it is "upworthy" by clicking on it, thus moving it "up" in your pile of things deemed "worthy" to read and look at online.

Recently, historian Jill Lepore turned a critical eye to the problem of using social media as an indicator of scholarly impact. She worries that publicity, for its own sake, will be taken as a measure of worth, and she cautions that if attention replaces citation as the author's compensation, we will all soon operate in a universe in which search engines that reward "nothing but outrageousness" (and cat videos) will determine scholarly merit.[27] She makes an excellent point here. We certainly don't mean for our discussion of altmetrics to suggest that "likes" or downloads should replace peer review. However, the expansion of digital technologies and the proliferation of scholarly work in a variety of formats signals that what "peer review" means is changing—and that can be a good thing.

One of the key insights in the British report by Wilsdon and colleagues is that excellence in research is multidimensional and changes over time, but that current measures often don't allow for this kind of variation. Indeed, our current measures are deeply flawed. While some regard the journal impact factor (JIF) as one of the highest standards of peer-review measurement, critics contend that it's as much a popularity measure as an Upworthy quiz—except slower. In fact, the JIF has been deemed to be so flawed that there is a movement afoot to have it eliminated from any and all evaluation measures. In 2012, a group of scholars, journal editors and publishers, scholarly societies, and research funders across a range of disciplines issued a declaration calling on the world scientific community to stop using JIF in evaluating research for funding, hiring, promotion, or institutional effectiveness. To date, over 12,500 individuals and 585 organizations have signed on to the San Francisco Declaration on Research Assessment (DORA) (http://www.ascb.org/dora/). The fact is there are no good ways to measure your work as a public scholar and make it count in ways that are legible across *all* institutions of higher education. Maybe that's a good thing, or maybe it's not, but it's where we are now.

Making a Difference as a Scholar

Scholars, particularly in the social sciences, are confident in talking about impact, just not when it comes to their own work. Sociologist Mark Granovetter describes the complex, nuanced ways that institutions have an impact upon the economy. In public health and medical sociology, scholars write confidently about how this or that social determinant has an impact on health. Even in the digital humanities, academics can explain to you the "impact of digitized collections on teaching and learning."[28] But we are much more reticent to talk about, or even consider, the impact our scholarship has on the world. Some might argue that this is because our impact is so very small that there's not much to talk about! But, at best, that claim represents a kind of false modesty; at worst, it underestimates the very privileged status that scholars hold in society. In 2013, just under 2 percent of the US population over the age of twenty-five held a PhD degree. Downplaying the way we can use our education may let us off the hook for making a difference.

The fact is digital technologies are changing what it means to be a scholar-activist. At least since 1999, activists and academics, two overlapping groups at times, have used social media to help stage social protests against globalization. Activists organized the Seattle protests against the World Trade Organization, known as the Battle in Seattle, online using Usenet, Internet Relay Chat channels, and electronic bulletin boards, thus eluding police surveillance. By 2005, blogging joined the front lines of activism.[29] At around the same time, many academics began scholarly blogs to engage in new forms of intellectual activism.

For example, Joe R. Feagin and Jessie Daniels's scholarly blog, *Racism Review*, offers a mix of current events, scholarly research, and insightful commentary in a noncommercial, ad-free space. The numbers who viewed the blog are notable: around two hundred thousand unique visitors each month, and an estimated 2.7 million visitors since the blog began. If the editors had a desire to sell advertising space on the blog, it is these larger numbers that would interest advertisers. Online advertisers will pay to reach a potential audience of hundreds of thousands of readers, and each click through an advertisement to a purchase equals more revenue. But Joe and Jessie were less interested in ad revenue than they were in making a difference. So, for them, the smaller numbers are a crucial set of metrics that suggest community formation. The 150 authors listed are often graduate students, early career researchers, and independent public scholars in other settings who looked to the blog as a place to try out being a public scholar. The ten thousand or so comments and subscribers to the blog speak to a sustained engagement in difficult issues with other scholars, and with a wider public, such as those in community groups, religious organizations, and high schools. And the seventeen hundred individual posts signal the knowledge production that is at the center of a scholarly blog like this one.

Racism Review **Blog Statistics, February 2016**

Individual blog posts	1,794
Comments from readers	10,846
Subscribers	10,754
Authors	150

Making a Difference outside the Academy

According to a recent survey, 92 percent of scholars surveyed said they wanted to have greater influence on policy.[30] That's a huge proportion of academics that want to have an impact. What's going on here? As human beings, we want to know that our lives matter, and that we have an impact upon the world, just like George Bailey. Many scholars, but certainly not all, want to know that the work they put so much time, training, money, and effort into matters in some way beyond the small circle of experts in their chosen field. As British astrophysicist Martin Rees says, "Almost all scientists want their work to have an impact beyond academia, commercial, societal, or broadly cultural, and are delighted when this happens. But they realize, as many administrators and politicians do not, that such successes cannot be planned for and are often best achieved by curiosity-motivated research."[31]

He's right that most academics want their work to have an impact beyond academia. The desire for our work to matter is a class-bound one, to be sure, in ways that may not be obvious. From a public health perspective, sanitation workers have possibly the most important jobs—perhaps more important than doctors for the general health of a city, for example—and they can certainly take comfort in the fact that they promote the health of large populations of people. It's harder for academics that trade in the currency of ideas to point to the impact of our work, but the desire is an existential one.

So, how do you make a difference outside the academy? Well, the first thing to do is insure that your life is not swallowed up by your job. Political scientist Robert Putnam tells us that we are no longer a society of people who join things, whether those are bowling teams or community boards. We're suffering for this lack of community, Putnam contends, because we aren't as connected to other people. While no one, to our knowledge, has done research on academics à la Putnam's *Bowling Alone* study, impressions suggest that a good many of us are so focused on our teaching and research that we spend very little time engaged in community or civic work.

Sociologist Kieran Healy muses about the academic culture that pillories any nonresearch activities as "frivolous nonsense" in an imagined (but not unimaginable) conversation between himself and a colleague:

You have time to watch television? I don't even own a TV. . . . You go jogging in the morning? How do you find the time? You have time to shower afterward? Personal grooming distracts from the research effort. You walk to the other end of the building to use the bathroom? I specifically requested that my office have the toilet seat model of the Aeron chair installed. A real time saver, that one. You have *small children*? Actually, why am I even wasting my time talking to you right now? Goodbye.[32]

Healy, whose early academic habits were formed in Ireland, sees this as a particularly American affectation, rooted in Puritanical values espoused by the likes of Ben Franklin ("early to bed and early to rise . . .") and middle-class understandings of the virtue of hard work. The neoliberal restructuring of higher education may mean that we are all becoming Ben Franklins. Increasingly, work that doesn't lead to a clear "payoff" in terms of that almighty metric, the peer-reviewed publication, is discouraged. It's not simply an American problem, of course, as we've seen in the example of the United Kingdom, where the speeded-up academy, some argue, is ascendant. Getting credit for one's accomplishments is important, to be sure. But protecting a zone of intellectual creativity and social commitment outside the sphere of measurement, which can't be quantified by an H-index, is important, too.

Another way of making a difference is to engage in a spirited defense of things you think are important outside and inside the academy—such as public funding for higher education, better working conditions for those at the lower echelons of the academic workforce—along with criticizing things you think are problematic. Today, scholars who engage in dissent are often dismissed as opinionated blowhards, ivory tower elitists, or as simply irrelevant. But as social scientists, we know that the knowledge we produce is rarely, if ever, value free. By going public, we can put our research to good use by unsettling power, troubling consensus, challenging common sense, and, enlivening the public sphere. And, like the fictional George Bailey, we might even be able to make a difference.

Acknowledgments

Arlene Stein:

When I was in graduate school at Berkeley long ago, the lucid writing and engaged scholarship of many of my professors inspired me, and continues to do so. I've also benefited from Jodi O'Brien's keen insights and smart provocations over our decades-long friendship. Thanks to the American Sociological Association for giving Jodi and me the opportunity to take over the editorial reins of *Contexts*, and to Karen Cerulo, Deborah Carr, and Lisa Iorillo at Rutgers for providing support and assistance.

I'd like to express thanks to Laurie Essig, Doug Hartmann, Angelique Haugerud, William Helmreich, Paul Hirschfield, Jim Jasper, and John Seery for offering feedback, and for discussing their work and the challenges of going public with me. Thanks, too, to many others whose words appear in these pages. Miriam Altschuler and Marlie Wasserman offered advice about the publishing world, and Ted Conover helped me think about the possibility of bridging journalistic and social science writing. Cynthia Chris, an accomplished writer herself, gave me editorial feedback and a comfortable place to rest my head.

Jessie and I owe thanks to Doug Mitchell at the University of Chicago Press, who understood the importance of this project from the start, expressed enthusiastic interest, and shepherded the manuscript to publication, along with Kyle Wagner and Mark Reschke. We would also like to thank several anonymous reviewers who helped us make the book much better.

Jessie Daniels:

As with any book project, this one would not have happened without a lot of enthusiasm, encouragement, and material support from other people not listed as authors. I want to start by thanking Arlene Stein for proposing this book project and inviting me to coauthor with her. Without that initial conversation over dumplings, this book would not exist.

We thank Howard Becker in the text, but I want to thank him again here because his terrific example of *Writing for Social Scientists* served as a guiding light for us in writing this book. I stand on the shoulders of two giants in the field of sociology: Joe Feagin and Patricia Hill Collins. Joe Feagin was once my dissertation advisor and now is so much more as a coeditor and collaborator at *Racism Review*. I am a public sociologist in large measure because of him. Patricia Hill Collins was once my postdoctoral supervisor. When I was turning a dissertation into a book, she wisely counseled me to "write a book undergraduates can read." She continues to guide through her example as an intellectual activist, through her writing, and through the work she cites.

I am grateful to have wonderful friends and colleagues who were willing to be interviewed for this book, including Alondra Nelson, Dustin Kidd, Lisa Wade, Douglas Hartmann, Zeynep Tufekci, Lester Andrist, and Nathan Palmer. In addition to interviews, we cited the public scholarship of other colleagues and I am grateful for them as well, including Tressie McMillan Cottom, Eric Anthony Grollman, Imani Perry, Patricia A. Matthew, and L'Heureux Lewis-McCoy. Finally, Jules Netherland read every word, as she always does, and offered a soft place to land when I needed one. For her, all my thanks are never enough.

Notes

Introduction

1. Nicholas Kristof, "Professors, We Need You!," *New York Times*, February 15, 2014, http://www.nytimes.com/2014/02/16/opinion/sunday/kristof-professors-we-need-you.html?_r=0.

2. Robyn Rodriguez, correspondence with the authors.

3. Howard Becker, "Some Words about Writing," *Writing on Writing*, Durham University, https://www.dur.ac.uk/writingacrossboundaries/writingonwriting/howardsbecker/.

4. Dan Meyer, "Stanford History Education Professor Sam Wineburg Learns to Tweet," *Dy/Dan Blog*, February 18, 2013, accessed February 28, 2016, http://blog.mrmeyer.com/2013/stanford-history-education-professor-sam-wineburg-learns-to-tweet/.

5. Robert Borofsky, "Defining Public Anthropology," *Center for a Public Anthropology*, May 11, 2011, accessed February 28, 2016, http://www.publicanthropology.org/public-anthropology/.

6. Angelique Haugerud, "Public Anthropology and the Financial Crisis," *Anthropology Today* 29, no. 6 (December 2013): 7.

7. Christopher Uggen and Michelle Inderbitzin, "The Price and the Promise of Citizenship: Extending the Vote to Nonincarcerated Felons," in *Contemporary Issues in Criminal Justice Policy: Policy Proposals from the American Society of*

Criminology Conference, ed. Natasha A. Frost, Joshua D. Freilich, and Todd R. Clear (Belmont, CA: Cengage/Wadsworth, 2010), 61–68.

8. Phil Cohen, "Quote That Sociologist, 124 in *The Times Edition*," *Family Inequality Blog*, https://familyinequality.wordpress.com/2014/02/20/quote-that -sociologist-124-in-the-times-edition/.

9. William Buxton and Stephen P. Turner, "From Education to Expertise: Sociology as a Profession," in *Sociology and Its Publics*, ed. Terence C. Halliday and Morris Janowitz (Berkeley: University of California Press, 1992): 373–408.

10. Ben Agger, *Public Sociology* (Boulder, CO: Rowman and Littlefield, 2000); Arlene Stein, "Discipline and Publish: Public Sociology in an Age of Professionalization," in *Bureaucratic Culture and Escalating Problems: Advancing the Sociological Imagination*, ed. David Knottnerus and Bernard Phillips (Boulder, CO: Paradigm Publishers, 2009).

11. Karen Sternheimer, "The Mediated Sociologist," *Contexts* (Spring 2014): 56–58.

12. Catherine Besteman and Hugh Gusterson, eds., *Why America's Top Pundits Are Wrong: Anthropologists Talk Back* (Berkeley: University of California Press, 2005).

13. Tamar Lewin, "Parents' Financial Support May Not Help College Grades," *New York Times*, January 14, 2013, http://www.nytimes.com/2013/01/15/education/ parents-financial-support-linked-to-college-grades.html?_r=0.

14. George Ritzer, *Introduction to Sociology* (Thousand Oaks, CA: Sage), 30.

15. Pepper Schwartz, "Stage Fright or Death Wish: Sociology in the Mass Media," *Contemporary Sociology* 27, no. 5 (1998): 439–45.

Chapter One

1. Arthur Kleinman, "Writing across Borders," *Writing on Writing*, Durham University, https://www.dur.ac.uk/writingacrossboundaries/writingonwriting/ arthurkleinman/.

2. Quotes from C. Wright Mills are from "On Intellectual Craftsmanship," appendix to *The Sociological Imagination* (New York: Oxford University Press, 1959). Additional quotes are from Katherine Mills and Pamela Mills, eds., *C. Wright Mills: Letters and Autobiographical Writings* (Berkeley: University of California Press, 2001).

3. George Saunders, Interview, Long Form podcast, January 15, 2014, accessed February 28, 2016, http://longform.org/posts/longform-podcast-75-george -saunders.

4. Patricia Hill Collins, *On Intellectual Activism* (Philadelphia: Temple University Press, 2012).

5. C. Wright Mills, *The Sociological Imagination* (New York: Oxford University Press, 1959).

6. Michael Billig, "Social Sciences and the Noun Problem," www.guardian.co
.uk/higher-education-network/blog/2013.

7. "On Being an Independent Sociologist of Culture: Sarah Thornton Answers
Ann Mullen's Questions," *ASA Culture Section Newsletter* 27, no. 1 (Summer 2015).

8. Arthur Frank, "Writing as a Form of Analysis," *Writing on Writing*, Durham
University, https://www.dur.ac.uk/writingacrossboundaries/writingonwriting/
arthurwfrank/.

9. Cheryl Brumley, "Academia and Storytelling Are Not Incompatible," http://
blogs.lse.ac.uk/impactofsocialsciences/2014/08/27/academic-storytelling-risk
-reduction/.

10. Ta-Nehisi Coates, "The Case for Reparations," *Atlantic*, June 2014.

11. Brumley, "Academia and Storytelling Are Not Incompatible."

Chapter Two

1. Tricia Hall, "Op-Ed and You," *New York Times*, October 13, 2013, http://www
.nytimes.com/2013/10/14/opinion/op-ed-and-you.html?_r=0.

2. Dalton Conley, "Out of the Tower and into the Fire: Op-Ed Tip Sheet for
Academics and Other Contemplative Creatures," http://andrewleigh.org/pdf/OpEd
_Tips_Conley.pdf.

3. Ibid.

4. Ruth Milkman, "A More Perfect Union," *New York Times*, June 30, 2005.

5. Jennifer Lena, "Why Hipsters Hate on Lana Del Rey," *Pacific Standard*, December 9, 2012, http://www.psmag.com/books-and-culture/lana-del-rey-hip-hop
-grunge-rick-ross-authentic-music-50442.

6. Ibid.

7. Personal communication with authors.

8. Paul Hirschfield, "Why Do American Cops Kill So Many Compared to European Cops?," *The Conversation*, November 25, 2015, accessed February 28, 2016,
https://theconversation.com/why-do-american-cops-kill-so-many-compared-to
-european-cops-49696.

9. Laura Hamilton and Elizabeth Armstrong, "The (Mis)Education of Monica
and Karen," *Contexts* 11, no. 4 (Fall 2012): 22–27, http://ctx.sagepub.com/content/
11/4/22.abstract.

Chapter Three

1. David Riesman, *The Lonely Crowd: A Study of the Changing American Character*
(New Haven, CT: Yale University Press, 1950).

2. Herbert Gans, "Best Sellers by Sociologists: An Exploratory Study," *Contemporary Sociology* 26, no. 2 (March 1997): 34–39.

3. Heidi N. Moore, "Why Is Thomas Piketty's 700-page Book a Bestseller?,"
The Guardian, September 21, 2014, accessed June 28, 2015, http://www.theguardian

.com/money/2014/sep/21/-sp-thomas-piketty-bestseller-why. David L. Swartz, "From Critical Sociology to Public Intellectual: Pierre Bourdieu and Politics," *Theory and Society* 32, nos. 5–6 (2003): 791–823. Sociologist Bryan Turner argues that British sociology, driven by the crisis of World War II, gave rise to a distinctive tradition of public intellectuals, including many Jewish immigrants, writing about social class, race, and gender; yet the transformation of the United Kingdom into a more affluent consumer society has marked a decline in such publicly engaged scholarship. See Bryan S. Turner, "British Sociology and Public Intellectuals: Consumer Society and Imperial Decline," *British Journal of Sociology* 57, no. 2 (2006): 169–88.

4. Robert Kuttner, "She Minds the Child, He Minds the Dog," *New York Times, Book Review*, June 25, 1989.

5. Eric Klinenberg, *Going Solo: The Extraordinary Rise and Surprising Appeal of Living Alone* (New York: Penguin Press, 2012), 123.

6. Robert Putnam, *Bowling Alone: The Collapse and Revival of American Community* (New York: Simon and Schuster, 2000).

7. Sudhir Venkatesh, *Gang Leader for a Day* (New York: Penguin, 2008), 59.

8. Alex Kotlowitz, "Deep Cover: Review of *On the Run*," *New York Times Book Review*, June 29, 2014, 14.

9. Barry Glassner, *The Culture of Fear: Why Americans Are Afraid of the Wrong Things; Crime, Drugs, Minorities, Teen Moms, Killer Kids, Mutant Microbes, Plane Crashes, Road Rage, and So Much More* (New York: Basic Books, 1999), xiii.

10. Ibid., 25

11. Ibid., 210.

12. See, for example, Joshua Gamson's *The Fabulous Sylvester: The Legend, the Music, the Seventies in San Francisco* (New York: Picador, 2006); William Helmreich, *The New York Nobody Knows: Walking 6,000 Miles in the City* (Princeton, NJ: Princeton University Press, 2015); Pepper Schwartz, *Everything You Know about Love and Sex Is Wrong* (New York: Perigee Books, 2001).

13. Joshua Gamson, *Modern Families: Stories of Extraordinary Journeys to Kinship* (New York: New York University Press, 2015); Phil Zuckerman, *Living the Secular Life: New Answers to Old Questions* (New York: Penguin, 2014).

14. Interview with Alondra Nelson, conducted by Jessie Daniels, August 2015.

15. Alane Mason, "Nine Tips for Academics Writing for a General Audience," http://wwnorton.tumblr.com/post/32954793512/nine-tips-for-academics-writing-for-a-general.

16. Gamson, *Modern Families*, 89.

17. Mason, *Nine Tips*.

18. See Jack Hart, *Storycraft: The Complete Guide to Writing Narrative Nonfiction* (Chicago: University of Chicago Press, 2012).

19. Theresa MacPhail, "The Art and Science of Finding Your Voice," *Chronicle of Higher Education*, August 8, 2014, 21.

20. Ilene Kalish, "Great Books Aren't Written, They're Re-Written," *Contexts* 12, no. 3 (August 11, 2013): 88.

21. Sudhir Venkatesh, "Writing Outside the (Sociological) Box," *Contexts* 13, no. 2 (2014): 92.

Chapter Four

1. Tomi Oladepo, "The Digital Academic, a Changing Culture—Interview (with Dr. Charlotte Mathieson," *Digital Media Culture*, October 21, 2014, accessed September 23, 2015, http://digimediaculture.com/2014/10/21/the-digital-academic-a -changing-culture-interview/.

2. Deborah Lupton, *Digital Sociology* (New York: Routledge, 2014).

3. Deborah Lupton, "'Feeling Better Connected': Academics' Use of Social Media," Canberra: News & Media Research Centre, University of Canberra (2014).

4. Jessie Daniels and Polly Thistlethwaite, *Being a Scholar Now* (New York: Policy Press, 2016).

5. Jessie Daniels and Joe R. Feagin, "The (Coming) Social Media Revolution in the Academy," *Fast Capitalism* 8, no. 2 (2011), http://www.uta.edu/huma/agger/ fastcapitalism/8_2/Daniels8_2.html.

6. Jason Priem, Kaitlin Costello, and Tyler Dzuba, "Prevalence and Use of Twitter among Scholars," in *Metrics: Symposium on Informetric and Scientometric Research* (2011), figshare, accessed August 22, 2015, http://dx.doi.org/10.6084/m9 .figshare.104629.

7. Eva Kassens-Noor, "Twitter as a Teaching Practice to Enhance Active and Informal Learning in Higher Education: The Case of Sustainable Tweets," *Active Learning in Higher Education* 13, no. 1 (2012): 9–21; Eileen Scanlon, "Scholarship in the Digital Age: Open Educational Resources, Publication and Public Engagement," *British Journal of Educational Technology* 45, no. 1 (2014): 12–23; George Veletsianos, "Higher Education Scholars' Participation and Practices on Twitter," *Journal of Computer Assisted Learning* 28, no. 4 (2012): 336–49; Jeffrey R. Young, "Teaching with Twitter: Not for the Faint of Heart," *Education Digest: Essential Readings Condensed for Quick Review* 75, no. 7 (2010): 9–12; Katrin Weller, Axel Bruns, Jean Burgess, Merja Mahrt, and Cornelius Puschmann, eds., *Twitter and Society* (New York: Peter Lang, 2013); Deborah Lupton, *Digital Sociology* (New York: Routledge, 2014); Bonnie Stewart, "In Abundance: Networked Participatory Practices as Scholarship," *International Review of Research in Open and Distributed Learning* 16, no. 3 (2015), http://www.irrodl.org/index.php/irrodl/article/view/ 2158/3343; Bonnie Stewart, "Open to Influence: What Counts as Academic Influence in Scholarly Networked Twitter Participation," *Learning, Media and Technology* 40, no. 3 (2015): 1–23.

8. Cathy N. Davidson, *The Future of Learning Institutions in a Digital Age* (Cambridge, MA: MIT Press, 2009).

9. Daniels and Thistlethwaite, *Being a Scholar in the Digital Era*.

10. Orvar Löfgren, "Routinising Research: Academic Skills in Analogue and Digital Worlds," *International Journal of Social Research Methodology* 17, no. 1 (2014): 73–86.

11. Kathleen Fitzpatrick, *Planned Obsolescence: Publishing, Technology and the Future of the Academy* (New York: New York University Press, 2011). The open peer-review site is available here: http://mcpress.media-commons.org/plannedobsolescence/.

12. Kathleen Fitzpatrick, "Networking the Field," *Planned Obsolescence*, January 10, 2010, accessed August 26, 2015, http://www.plannedobsolescence.net/networking-the-field/.

13. Fitzpatrick, *Planned Obsolescence*.

14. Emily Ford, "Defining and Characterizing Open Peer Review: A Review of the Literature," *Journal of Scholarly Publishing* 44, no. 4 (2013): 311–26.

15. Daniels and Thistlethwaite, *Being a Scholar in the Digital Era*.

16. Lupton, *Digital Sociology*.

17. "Interview: Danielle Henderson, Creator of Feminist Ryan Gosling," *A.V. Club*, January 11, 2012, accessed August 22, 2015, http://www.avclub.com/article/danielle-henderson-creator-of-feminist-ryan-goslin-67419.

18. Danielle Henderson, *Feminist Ryan Gosling: Feminist Theory (as Imagined) from Your Favorite Sensitive Movie Dude* (New York: Running Press, 2012).

19. Owen Williams, "The 18 Best Blogging and Publishing Platforms on the Internet Today," *The Next Web*, May 11, 2015, http://thenextweb.com/businessapps/2015/05/11/the-18-best-blogging-and-publishing-platforms-on-the-internet-today/.

20. Howard Rheingold, "Twitter Literacy (I Refuse to Make Up a Twittery Name for It)," *SFGate*, May 11, 2009, accessed August 22, 2015, http://blog.sfgate.com/rheingold/2009/05/11/twitter-literacy-i-refuse-to-make-up-a-twittery-name-for-it/.

21. Bonnie Stewart, "In Abundance: Networked Participatory Practices as Scholarship," *International Review of Research in Open and Distributed Learning* (2015), accessed June 28, 2015, http://www.irrodl.org/index.php/irrodl/article/view/2158/3343.

Chapter Five

1. Interview with Alondra Nelson, conducted by Jessie Daniels, September 8, 2015.

2. Interview with Nathan Palmer, conducted by Jessie Daniels, September 8, 2015.

3. Interview with Dustin Kidd, conducted by Jessie Daniels, September 21, 2015.

4. Lisa Wade and Gwen Sharp, "Sociological Images Blogging as Public Sociol-

ogy," *Social Science Computer Review* 31, no. 2 (2013): 221–28; interview with Lisa Wade, September 4, 2015.

5. Michelle Alexander, *The New Jim Crow: Mass Incarceration in the Era of Colorblindness* (New York: The New Press, 2010), 15.

6. George Ritzer, "Who's a Public Intellectual?," *British Journal of Sociology* 57, no. 2 (2006): 209–13.

7. Ibid.

8. Interview with Letta Wren Page, conducted by Jessie Daniels, September 15, 2015.

9. Morgane Richardson, "Interview with PJ Rey and Nathan Jurgenson," *JustPublics@365*, March 1, 2013, accessed August 26, 2015, http://justpublics365 .commons.gc.cuny.edu/2013/03/01/an-interview-with-pj-nathan-founders-of -ttw13/.

10. Phil Agre, "Networking on the Network," March 20, 2002, accessed June 28, 2015, http://vlsicad.ucsd.edu/Research/Advice/network.html.

11. Lester Andrist, Valerie Chepp, Paul Dean, and Michael V. Miller, "Toward a Video Pedagogy: A Teaching Typology with Learning Goals," *Teaching Sociology* 42, no. 3 (2014): 196–206, doi:10.1177/0092055X14524962.

12. Interview with Lester Andrist, conducted by Jessie Daniels, August 24, 2015.

13. Andrist, Chepp, Dean, and Miller, "Toward a Video Pedagogy."

14. Howard Rheingold, *Net Smart: How to Thrive Online* (Cambridge, MA: MIT Press, 2012); Seth Godin, *Tribes: We Need You to Lead Us* (New York: Penguin, 2008)

15. Interview with Nate Palmer, conducted by Jessie Daniels, September 8, 2015.

16. Interview with Lisa Wade, conducted by Jessie Daniels, September 4, 2015.

17. Angèle Christin, "Just Counting Clicks? How Web Analytics Shape the Market for Online News," paper presented at Digital Sociology Mini-Conference, Eastern Sociological Society, February 27, 2015.

18. Interview with Nate Palmer, conducted by Jessie Daniels, September 8, 2015.

19. Interview with Dustin Kidd, conducted by Jessie Daniels, September 21, 2015.

20. Imani Perry, "The New Black Public Intellectual," *Chronicle of Higher Education*, June 6, 2010, accessed June 28, 2015, https://chronicle.com/article/The-New -Black-Public/65744/.

21. Jessie Daniels, "Interview: Brian Stoudt and Maria Torre," *JustPublics@365*, November 13, 2016, accessed August 22, 2015, http://justpublics365.commons.gc .cuny.edu/2013/11/06/interview-morris-justice-project/.

22. Julie Netherland, "Tips for Academics Who Want to Work with Policy Makers," *JustPublics@365*, October 24, 2013, accessed June 28, 2015, http://

justpublics365.commons.gc.cuny.edu/2013/10/24/tips-academics-want-to
-engage-policymakers/.

23. Jim Dwyer, "Whites Smoke Pot, Blacks Get Arrested," *New York Times*,
December 22, 2009, accessed September 23, 2015, http://www.nytimes.com/2009/
12/23/nyregion/23about.html.

Chapter Six

1. Jane Ward, *Not Gay: Sex between Straight White Men* (New York: New York
University Press, 2015).

2. Interview with Lisa Wade, conducted by Jessie Daniels, September 2015.

3. Terrell Jermaine Starr, "The Unbelievable Harassment Black Women
Face Daily on Twitter," *Alternet*, September 16, 2014, accessed on June 28, 2015,
http://www.alternet.org/unbelievable-harassment-black-women-face-daily
-twitter.

4. Katia Hetter, "Online Fury over Boston University Professor's Tweets on
Race," *CNN*, May 13, 2015, accessed June 28, 2015, http://www.cnn.com/2015/05/
13/living/feat-boston-university-saida-grundy-race-tweets/.

5. Scott Jaschik, "The Professor Who Wasn't Fired," *Inside Higher Ed*, July 1,
2015, accessed August 25, 2015, https://www.insidehighered.com/news/2015/07/
01/twitter-explodes-false-reports-u-memphis-fired-professor-why.

6. Scott Jaschik, "Saida Grundy, Moving Forward," *Inside Higher Ed*, August 24,
2015, accessed August 25, 2015, https://www.insidehighered.com/news/2015/08/
24/saida-grundy-discusses-controversy-over-her-comments-twitter-her-career
-race-and.

7. Arlene Stein, *The Stranger Next Door: The Story of a Small Community's Battle
over Sex, Faith, and Civil Rights* (Boston: Beacon, 2001).

8. For more on the controversy, see Arlene Stein, "Sex, Truths, and Audiotape:
Anonymity and the Effects of Exposure in Public Ethnography," *Journal of Contemporary Ethnography* 39, no. 5 (October 2010): 554–68.

9. Benjamin Geer, "Autonomy and Symbolic Capital in an Academic Social
Movement: The March 9 Group in Egypt," *European Journal of Turkish Studies:
Social Sciences on Contemporary Turkey* 17 (2013), accessed August 25, 2015, http://
ejts.revues.org/4780.

10. Dwayne Betts, "The Stoop Isn't the Jungle," *Slate*, July 10, 2014, accessed
August 22, 2015, http://www.slate.com/articles/news_and_politics/jurisprudence/
2014/07/alice_goffman_s_on_the_run_she_is_wrong_about_black_urban_life
.single.html.

11. Christina Sharpe, "Black Life—Annotated," *The New Inquiry*, August 8,
2014, accessed August 22, 2015, http://thenewinquiry.com/essays/black-life
-annotated/.

12. Paul Campos, "Alice Goffman's Implausible Ethnography," *Chronicle of*

Higher Education, August 21, 2015, accessed August 26, 2015, http://chronicle.com/article/Alice-Goffmans-Implausible-/232491/.

13. Steven Lubet, "Ethics on the Run: Review of *On the Run: Fugitive Life in an American City* by Alice Goffman," *New Rambler Review*, 2015, accessed August 25, 2015, http://newramblerreview.com/book-reviews/law/ethics-on-the-run.

14. Gideon Lewis-Kraus, "The Trials of Alice Goffman," *New York Times*, January 12, 2016, http://www.nytimes.com/2016/01/17/magazine/the-trials-of-alice-goffman.html.

15. Lubet, "Ethics on the Run."

16. Interview with Lisa Wade, conducted by Jessie Daniels, September 2015.

17. Elizabeth Garone, "Can Social Media Get You Fired?," *BBC*, November 3, 2014, accessed August 22, 2015, http://www.bbc.com/capital/story/20130626-can-social-media-get-you-fired.

18. Adam Weinstein, "FSU Lecturer Loses Job over Rant against 'Filthy Rodent Muslims,'" *Gawker*, December 10, 2014, accessed August 26, 2015, http://gawker.com/fsu-lecturer-loses-job-over-rant-against-filthy-rodent-1669244536.

19. Derek Kinner, "FSU Instructor Resigns after Folio Weekly Asks about Racist Emails," *Folio Weekly*, December 8, 2014, accessed August 26, 2015, http://folioweekly.com/FSU-INSTRUCTOR-RESIGNS-AFTER-FOLIO-WEEKLY-ASKS-ABOUT-RACIST-FACEBOOK-POSTS,11706.

20. Weinstein, "FSU Lecturer Loses Job."

21. Jaschik, "Firing a Faculty Blogger," *Inside Higher Ed*, February 5, 2015, accessed August 26, 2015, https://www.insidehighered.com/news/2015/02/05/marquette-moves-fire-controversial-faculty-blogger.

22. Robert Mackey, "Professor's Angry Tweets on Gaza Cost Him His Job," *New York Times*, September 12, 2014, accessed August 26, 2015, http://www.nytimes.com/2014/09/13/world/middleeast/professors-angry-tweets-on-gaza-cost-him-a-job.html.

23. John K. Wilson, "How Money Mattered in the Salaita Case," *Academe Blog*, January 6, 2015, accessed August 26, 2015, http://academeblog.org/2015/01/06/how-money-mattered-in-the-salaita-case/.

24. Scott Jaschik, "The Emails on Salaita," *Inside Higher Ed*, August 25, 2014, accessed August 26, 2015, https://www.insidehighered.com/news/2014/08/25/u-illinois-officials-defend-decision-deny-job-scholar-documents-show-lobbying.

25. Peter Schmidt, "Twitter Casualty," *Chronicle of Higher Education*, December 15, 2014, accessed August 26, 2015, http://www.chroniclecareers.com/article/2014-INFLUENCE-LIST-TWITTER/150853/#sthash.ke2YsJ6P.dpuf.

26. Quoted in Mark Carrigan, "Life in the Accelerated Academy: Anxiety Thrives, Demands Intensify and Metrics Hold the Tangled Web Together," *LSE Impact Blog*, April 7, 2015, accessed August 22, 2015, http://blogs.lse.ac.uk/impactofsocialsciences/2015/04/07/life-in-the-accelerated-academy-carrigan/.

27. Michael Burawoy, "Redefining the Public University: Developing an Analytical Framework," Transformations in the Public Sphere, Social Science Research Council, accessed August 22, 2015, http://publicsphere.ssrc.org/burawoy -redefining-the-public-university/.

28. Cheryl Brumley, "Academia and Storytelling Are Not Incompatible," *LSE Impact Blog*, August 27, 2014, accessed August 22, 2015, http://blogs.lse.ac.uk/ impactofsocialsciences/2014/08/27/academic-storytelling-risk-reduction/.

29. Henry Giroux, *Neoliberalism's War on Higher Education* (Chicago: Haymarket Books, 2014).

30. Brumley, "Academia and Storytelling."

31. Katrina vanden Heuvel, "Jenny McCarthy's Vaccination Fear-Mongering and the Cult of False Equivalence," *Nation*, July 22, 2013, accessed August 22, 2015, http://www.thenation.com/article/jenny-mccarthys-vaccination-fear-mongering -and-cult-false-equivalence/.

32. Jaschik, "The Emails on Salaita."

33. Garone, "Can Social Media Get You Fired?".

34. danah boyd, "Making Sense of Privacy and Publicity," South by Southwest, Austin, Texas, March 13, 2010, accessed August 22, 2015, http://www.danah.org/ papers/talks/2010/SXSW2010.html.

35. danah boyd, *It's Complicated: The Social Lives of Networked Teens* (New Haven, CT: Yale University Press, 2014).

36. Dani Shapiro, "Memoir Is Not a Status Update," *New Yorker*, August 18, 2014, accessed August 22, 2015, http://www.newyorker.com/culture/cultural -comment/memoir-status-update.

37. Tressie McMillan Cottom, "Everything but the Burden: Publics, Public Scholarship, and Institutions," *Tressiemc Blog*, May 12, 2015, accessed August 22, 2015, http://tressiemc.com/2015/05/12/everything-but-the-burden-publics-public -scholarship-and-institutions/.

38. Facebook invitation, reading at Skylight Books, Los Angeles, September 8, 2015.

39. Barry Glassner, *The Culture of Fear: Why Americans Are Afraid of the Wrong Things; Crime, Drugs, Minorities, Teen Moms, Killer Kids, Mutant Microbes, Plane Crashes, Road Rage, and So Much More* (New York: Basic Books, 2010).

40. Nick Wingfield, "Feminist Critics of Video Games Facing Threats in 'Gamergate' Campaign," *New York Times*, October 15, 2014, accessed August 22, 2015, http://www.nytimes.com/2014/10/16/technology/gamergate-women-video -game-threats-anita-sarkeesian.html.

41. Ibid.

42. Jessie Daniels, *Cyber Racism* (Lanham, MD: Rowman & Littlefield, 2009), 61.

43. Danielle Citron, *Hate Crimes in Cyberspace* (Cambridge, MA: Harvard University Press, 2014).

44. Soraya Chemaly, "'Hate Crimes in Cyberspace' Author: 'Everyone Is at

Risk, from Powerful Celebrities to Ordinary People,'" *Salon*, September 2, 2014, accessed August 22, 2015, http://www.salon.com/2014/09/02/hate_crimes_in _cyberspace_author_everyone_is_at_risk_from_the_most_powerful_celebrity_to _the_ordinary_person/.

45. Sarah Lai Stirland, "How a Trio of Feminists Persuaded Facebook to Unfriend Rape 'Humor' Groups," *TechPresident*, May 30, 2013, accessed August 22, 2015, http://techpresident.com/news/23945/how-trio-feminists-persuaded -facebook-unfriend-rape-humor-groups.

Chapter Seven

1. Madeline Cohen, Maura A. Smale, Jill Cirasella, Cynthia Tobar, and Jessie Daniels, "Speaking as One: Supporting Open Access with Departmental Resolutions," *Journal of Librarianship and Scholarly Communication* 2, no. 1 (2013), accessed June 28, 2015, http://dx.doi.org/10.7710/2162–3309.1099.

2. Anthea Butler, Plenary, Summit on Reimagining Scholarly Communication in the Digital Era, JustPublics@365, New York, March 6, 2013.

3. Personal communication with the authors, August 28, 2015.

4. Patricia Matthew, "@triciamatthew 4 associate professor," *Written/Unwritten Blog*, July 6, 2014, accessed June 28, 2015, https://writtenunwritten.wordpress .com/2014/07/06/triciamatthew-4-associate-professor/.

5. Open Access Institutional Repositories: A Briefing Paper, 2009, Liege, Belgium, Enabling Open Scholarship (EOS), accessed June 28, 2015, http://www .openscholarship.org/upload/docs/application/pdf/2009–09/open_access_ institutional_repositories.pdf.

6. Harvard University Library, Office of Scholarly Communication, "Open Access Policies," accessed June 28, 2015, https://osc.hul.harvard.edu/policies.

7. A preprint is usually the last version of the paper the author submitted to a journal, saved as a .pdf or .doc file, with "Preprint Version: Author Name, Dated August 22, 2015" in the header of the top left margin.

8. Julie E. Cohen, *Configuring the Networked Self: Code, and the Play of Everyday Practice* (New Haven, CT: Yale University Press, 2012), accessed June 28, 2015, http://www.juliecohen.com/page5.php; danah boyd, *It's Complicated: The Social Lives of Teens* (New Haven, CT: Yale University Press, 2014), accessed June 28, 2015, http://www.danah.org/books/ItsComplicated.pdf.

9. Shawnta Smith-Cruz, Polly Thistlethwaite, and Jessie Daniels, "Open Scholarship for Open Education: Building the JustPublics@365 POOC," *Journal of Library Innovation* 5, no. 2 (2014): 15, accessed June 28, 2015, http://www .libraryinnovation.org/article/view/370.

10. Emily VanBuren, "Should You Blog Your Dissertation Research?," *Grad Hacker Blog*, *IHE*, May 24, 2014, accessed June 28, 2015, https://www .insidehighered.com/blogs/gradhacker/open-thread-should-you-blog-your -dissertation-research.

11. Paulo Coelho, "Why I Pirate My Own Books," *Paulo Coelho's Blog*, February 7, 2008, accessed June 28, 2015, http://paulocoelhoblog.com/2008/02/07/paulo-coelho-why-i-pirate-my-own-books/.

12. Rebecca Schuman, "Why Did This Marxist Philosopher Plagiarize a White Supremacist Magazine?," *Slate*, July 14, 2014, accessed June 28, 2015, http://www.slate.com/blogs/browbeat/2014/07/14/slavoj_zizek_plagiarized_white_supremacist_magazine_american_renaissance.html.

13. Yochai Benkler, "Sharing Nicely: On Shareable Goods and the Emergence of Sharing as a Modality of Economic Production," *Yale Law Journal* 114 (2004): 273–358.

14. Deborah Lupton, *Digital Sociology* (New York: Routledge, 2014), 30.

15. Ann Okerson and Clifford Lynch, "Pondering the Digital Dilemma: A Personal Reflection," *Against the Grain* 12, no. 3 (2013): 20.

16. Jessie Daniels, "Cloaked Websites: Propaganda, Cyber-Racism and Epistemology in the Digital Era," *New Media & Society* 11, no. 5 (2009): 659–83.

17. Lawrence Lessig, *The Future of Ideas: The Fate of the Commons in a Connected World* (New York: Vintage, 2002).

18. Jason Priem, Dario Taraborelli, Paul Groth, and Cameron Neylon, "Altmetrics: Manifesto," *Altmetrics Blog*, October 26, 2010, accessed June 28, 2015, http://altmetrics.org/manifesto.

19. Heather Piwowar, "Altmetrics: Value All Research Products," *Nature* 493 (January 10, 2013): 159, http://www.nature.com/nature/journal/v493/n7431/full/493159a.html.

20. Xin Shuai, Alberto Pepe, and Johan Bollen, "How the Scientific Community Reacts to Newly Submitted Preprints: Article Downloads, Twitter Mentions, and Citations," *PLoS ONE* 7, no. 11 (2012): e47523, accessed August 22, 2015, doi:10.1371/journal.pone.0047523.

21. James Wilsdon, Liz Allen, Eleonora Belfiore, Philip Campbell, Stephen Curry, Steven Hill, Richard Jones, et al., "The Metric Tide: Report of the Independent Review of the Role of Metrics in Research Assessment and Management," *Digital Education Resource Archive*, July 16, 2015, accessed August 28, 2105, http://dera.ioe.ac.uk/23424/.

22. Manuel Pastor, J. Ito, and Rachel Rosner, "Transactions—Transformations—Translations: Metrics That Matter for Building, Scaling, and Funding Social Movements," Report (Los Angeles: USC Program for Environmental and Regional Equity, 2011), accessed June 28, 2015, http://bolderadvocacy.org/reco-resource/transactions-transformations-translations-metrics-that-matter-for-building-scaling-and-funding-social-movements.

23. Douglas Howard, "A Teaching Career in Fragments," *Chronicle of Higher Education*, February 24, 2014, accessed June 28, 2015, http://chronicle.com/article/A-Teaching-Career-in-Fragments/144911.

24. Mark McGuire, "The Difficulty in Rating Transformational Experiences,"

HASTAC Blog, February 8, 2014, accessed June 28, 2015, https://www.hastac.org/blogs/markmcguire/2014/02/08/difficulty-rating-transformational-experiences.

25. John Holmwood, "Death by Metrics," *Global Dialogue: Newsletter for the International Sociological Association*, October 30, 2013, accessed August 28, 2015, http://isa-global-dialogue.net/death-by-metrics/.

26. Mark Carrigan, "Life in the Accelerated Academy," *LSE Impact Blog*, April 7, 2015, accessed June 28, 2015, http://blogs.lse.ac.uk/impactofsocialsciences/2015/04/07/life-in-the-accelerated-academy-carrigan/.

27. Jill Lepore, "The New Economy of Letters," *Chronicle of Higher Education*, September 3, 2013, accessed June 28, 2015, http://chronicle.com/article/The-New-Economy-of-Letters/141291/.

28. Simon Tanner, "The Value and Impact of Digitized Resources for Learning, Teaching, Research and Enjoyment," in *Evaluating and Measuring the Value, Use and Impact of Digital Collections*, ed. Lorna Hughes (London: Facet Publishing, 2011), 103–20.

29. Richard Kahn and Douglas Kellner, "New Media and Internet Activism: From the 'Battle of Seattle' to Blogging," *New Media & Society* 6, no. 1 (2004): 87–95.

30. Beth McNair, "Social Scientists Seek New Ways to Influence Public Policy," *Chronicle of Higher Education*, April 30, 2013, accessed June 28, 2015, http://chronicle.com/article/Social-Scientists-Seek-New/141305.

31. Aisha Labi, "Researchers Resist Pressure to Show Impact of Their Work," *Chronicle of Higher Education*, February 9, 2014, accessed June 28, 2015, http://chronicle.com/article/Researchers-Resist-Pressure-to/144533/.

32. Kieran Healy, "On Wasting One's Time," *Kiernan Healy Blog*, February 7, 2008, accessed August 28, 2015, http://kieranhealy.org/blog/archives/2008/02/07/on-wasting-ones-time/.

Bibliography

Agger, Ben. *Public Sociology.* Boulder: Rowman and Littlefield, 2000.

Agre, Phil. "Networking on the Network." March 20, 2002. Accessed February 28, 2016. http://vlsicad.ucsd.edu/Research/Advice/network.html.

Alexander, Michelle. *The New Jim Crow: Mass Incarceration in the Era of Colorblindness.* New York: The New Press, 2010.

Andrist, Lester, Valerie Chepp, Paul Dean, and Michael V. Miller. "Toward a Video Pedagogy: A Teaching Typology with Learning Goals." *Teaching Sociology* 42, no. 3 (2014): 196–206.

Becker, Howard. "Some Words about Writing." Durham University, Department of Anthropology, Writing across Boundaries, n.d. Accessed February 28, 2016. https://www.dur.ac.uk/writingacrossboundaries/writingonwriting/howardsbecker/.

———. *Writing for Social Scientists: How to Start and Finish Your Thesis, Book, or Article.* Chicago: University of Chicago Press, 1986.

Benkler, Yochai. "Sharing Nicely: On Shareable Goods and the Emergence of Sharing as a Modality of Economic Production." *Yale Law Journal* 114 (2004): 273–358.

Besteman, Catherine, and Hugh Gusterson, eds. *Why America's Top Pundits Are Wrong: Anthropologists Talk Back.* Berkeley: University of California Press, 2005.

Betts, Dwayne. "The Stoop Isn't the Jungle." *Slate*, July 10, 2014. Accessed

February 28, 2016. http://www.slate.com/articles/news_and_politics/
jurisprudence/2014/07/alice_goffman_s_on_the_run_she_is_wrong_about
_black_urban_life.single.html.

Billig, Michael. "Social Sciences and the Noun Problem." *The Guardian*, July 11,
2013. Accessed February 28, 2015. http://www.guardian.co.uk/higher
-education-network/blog/2013.

Borofsky, Robert. "Defining Public Anthropology." *Center for a Public Anthropology*,
May 11, 2011. Accessed February 28, 2016. http://www.publicanthropology
.org/public-anthropology/.

boyd, danah. *It's Complicated: The Social Lives of Networked Teens*. New Haven, CT:
Yale University Press, 2014.

———. "Making Sense of Privacy and Publicity." South by Southwest, Austin,
Texas, March 13, 2010. Accessed February 28, 2016. http://www.danah.org/
papers/talks/2010/SXSW2010.html.

Brumley, Cheryl. "Academia and Storytelling Are Not Incompatible." *LSE Impact
Blog*, August 27, 2014. Accessed February 28, 2016. http://blogs.lse.ac.uk/
impactofsocialsciences/2014/08/27/academic-storytelling-risk-reduction/.

Burawoy, Michael. "Redefining the Public University: Developing an Analytical
Framework." Transformations in the Public Sphere, Social Science Research
Council. Accessed February 28, 2016. http://publicsphere.ssrc.org/burawoy
-redefining-the-public-university.

Butler, Anthea. Plenary address, Summit on Reimagining Scholarly Communication in the Digital Era, JustPublics@365, The Graduate Center, CUNY, New
York, March 6, 2013.

Buxton, William, and Stephen P. Turner. "From Education to Expertise: Sociology
as a Profession." In *Sociology and Its Publics*, ed. Terence C. Halliday and Morris
Janowitz, 373–408. Berkeley: University of California Press, 1992.

Campos, Paul. "Alice Goffman's Implausible Ethnography." *Chronicle of Higher
Education*, August 21, 2015. Accessed February 28, 2016. http://chronicle.com/
article/Alice-Goffmans-Implausible-/232491/.

Carrigan, Mark. "Life in the Accelerated Academy: Anxiety Thrives, Demands Intensify and Metrics Hold the Tangled Web Together." *LSE Impact Blog*, April 7, 2015. Accessed February 28, 2016. http://blogs.lse.ac
.uk/impactofsocialsciences/2015/04/07/life-in-the-accelerated-academy
-carrigan/.

Chemaly, Soraya. "'Hate Crimes in Cyberspace' Author: 'Everyone Is at Risk, from
Powerful Celebrities to Ordinary People.'" *Salon*, September 2, 2014. Accessed
February 28, 2016. http://www.salon.com/2014/09/02/hate_crimes_in
_cyberspace_author_everyone_is_at_risk_from_the_most_powerful_celebrity
_to_the_ordinary_person/.

Christin, Angèle. "Just Counting Clicks? How Web Analytics Shape the Market for

Online News." Paper presented at Digital Sociology Mini-Conference, Eastern Sociological Society, February 27, 2015.

Citron, Danielle. *Hate Crimes in Cyberspace*. Cambridge, MA: Harvard University Press, 2014.

Coates, Ta-Nehisi. "The Case for Reparations." *Atlantic*, June 2014. Accessed February 28, 2016. http://www.theatlantic.com/magazine/archive/2014/06/the -case-for-reparations/361631/.

Coelho, Paulo. "Why I Pirate My Own Books." *Paulo Coelho's Blog*, February 7, 2008. Accessed February 28, 2016. http://paulocoelhoblog.com/2008/02/07/ paulo-coelho-why-i-pirate-my-own-books.

Cohen, Julie E. *Configuring the Networked Self: Code, and the Play of Everyday Practice*. New Haven, CT: Yale University Press, 2012. Accessed February 28, 2016. http://www.juliecohen.com/page5.php.

Cohen, Madeline, Maura A. Smale, Jill Cirasella, Cynthia Tobar, and Jessie Daniels. "Speaking as One: Supporting Open Access with Departmental Resolutions." *Journal of Librarianship and Scholarly Communication* 2, no. 1 (2013). Accessed February 28, 2016. http://dx.doi.org/10.7710/2162–3309.1099.

Cohen, Philip. "Quote That Sociologist, 124 in *The Times* Edition." *Family Inequality Blog*, February 10, 2014. Accessed February 28, 2016. https://familyinequality .wordpress.com/2014/02/20/quote-that-sociologist-124-in-the-times -edition/.

Collins, Patricia Hill. *On Intellectual Activism*. Philadelphia: Temple University Press, 2012.

Conover, Ted. *Newjack: Guarding Sing Sing*. New York: Vintage, 2001.

Cottom, Tressie McMillan. "Everything but the Burden: Publics, Public Scholarship, and Institutions." *Tressiemc Blog*, May 12, 2015. Accessed February 28, 2016. http://tressiemc.com/2015/05/12/everything-but-the-burden-publics -public-scholarship-and-institutions/.

Daniels, Jessie. "Cloaked Websites: Propaganda, Cyber-Racism and Epistemology in the Digital Era." *New Media & Society* 11, no. 5 (2009): 659–83.

———. *Cyber Racism: White Supremacy Online and the New Attack on Civil Rights*. Lanham, MD: Rowman & Littlefield, 2009.

———. "Interview: Brian Stoudt and Maria Torre." *JustPublics@365*, November 13, 2016. Accessed February 28, 2016. http://justpublics365.commons.gc.cuny .edu/2013/11/06/interview-morris-justice-project/.

Daniels, Jessie, and Joe R. Feagin. "The (Coming) Social Media Revolution in the Academy." *Fast Capitalism* 8, no. 2 (2011). Accessed February 28, 2016. http:// www.uta.edu/huma/agger/fastcapitalism/8_2/Daniels8_2.html.

Daniels, Jessie, and Polly Thistlethwaite. *Being a Scholar in the Digital Era: Transforming Scholarly Practice for the Public Good*. New York: Policy Press, 2016.

Davidson, Cathy N., and David Theo Goldberg. *The Future of Learning Institutions in a Digital Age*. Cambridge, MA: MIT Press, 2009.

Duneier, Mitchell. *Sidewalk*. New York: Farrar, Strauss and Giroux, 2000.

Dwyer, Jim. "Whites Smoke Pot, Blacks Get Arrested." *New York Times*, December 22, 2009. Accessed February 28, 2016. http://www.nytimes.com/2009/12/23/nyregion/23about.html.

Ehrenreich, Barbara. *Nickel and Dimed: On Not Getting by in America*. New York: Picador, 2002.

Fitzpatrick, Kathleen. *Planned Obsolescence: Publishing, Technology and the Future of the Academy*. New York: New York University Press, 2011.

Ford, Emily. "Defining and Characterizing Open Peer Review: A Review of the Literature." *Journal of Scholarly Publishing* 44, no. 4 (2013): 311–26.

Frank, Arthur. "Writing as a Form of Analysis." Durham University, Department of Anthropology, Writing across Boundaries, n.d. Accessed February 28, 2016. https://www.dur.ac.uk/writingacrossboundaries/writingonwriting/arthurwfrank/.

Gamson, Joshua. *The Fabulous Sylvester: The Legend, the Music, the Seventies in San Francisco*. New York: Picador, 2006.

———. *Modern Families: Stories of Extraordinary Journeys to Kinship*. New York: New York University Press, 2015.

Gans, Herbert. "Best Sellers by Sociologists: An Exploratory Study." *Contemporary Sociology* 26, no. 2 (March 1997): 34–39.

Garone, Elizabeth. "Can Social Media Get You Fired?" *BBC*, November 3, 2014. Accessed February 28, 2016. http://www.bbc.com/capital/story/20130626-can-social-media-get-you-fired.

Geer, Benjamin. "Autonomy and Symbolic Capital in an Academic Social Movement: The March 9 Group in Egypt." *European Journal of Turkish Studies: Social Sciences on Contemporary Turkey* 17 (2013). Accessed February 28, 2016. http://ejts.revues.org/4780.

Giroux, Henry. *Neoliberalism's War on Higher Education*. Chicago: Haymarket Books, 2014.

Gladwell, Malcolm. *The Tipping Point*. New York: Back Bay, 2002.

Glassner, Barry. *The Culture of Fear: Why Americans Are Afraid of the Wrong Things; Crime, Drugs, Minorities, Teen Moms, Killer Kids, Mutant Microbes, Plane Crashes, Road Rage, and So Much More*. New York: Basic Books, 1999.

Godin, Seth. *Tribes: We Need You to Lead Us*. New York: Penguin, 2008.

Goffman, Alice. *On the Run: Fugitive Life in an American City*. Chicago: University of Chicago Press, 2014.

Hall, Tricia. "Op-Ed and You." *New York Times*, October 13, 2013. Accessed February 28, 2016. http://www.nytimes.com/2013/10/14/opinion/op-ed-and-you.html?_r=0.

Hamilton, Laura, and Elizabeth Armstrong. "The (Mis)Education of Monica and Karen." *Contexts* 11, no. 4 (Fall 2012): 22–27.

Hart, Jack. *Storycraft: The Complete Guide to Writing Narrative Nonfiction.* Chicago: University of Chicago Press, 2012.

Harvard University Library, Office of Scholarly Communication. "Open Access Policies." Accessed June 28, 2015. https://osc.hul.harvard.edu/policies.

Haugerud, Angelique. "Public Anthropology and the Financial Crisis." *Anthropology Today* 29, no. 6 (December 2013): 7.

Healy, Kieran. "On Wasting One's Time." *Kiernan Healy Blog*, February 7, 2008. Accessed February 28, 2016. http://kieranhealy.org/blog/archives/2008/02/07/on-wasting-ones-time/.

Helmreich, William. *The New York Nobody Knows: Walking 6,000 Miles in the City.* Princeton, NJ: Princeton University Press, 2015.

Henderson, Danielle. *Feminist Ryan Gosling: Feminist Theory (as Imagined) from Your Favorite Sensitive Movie Dude.* New York: Running Press, 2012.

Hetter, Katia. "Online Fury over Boston University Professor's Tweets on Race." *CNN*, May 13, 2015. Accessed February 28, 2016. http://www.cnn.com/2015/05/13/living/feat-boston-university-saida-grundy-race-tweets/.

Hirschfield, Paul. "Why Do American Cops Kill So Many Compared to European Cops?" *The Conversation*, November 25, 2015. Accessed February 28, 2016. https://theconversation.com/why-do-american-cops-kill-so-many-compared-to-european-cops-49696.

Hochschild, Arlie. *The Second Shift.* New York: Avon, 1997.

Holmwood, John. "Death by Metrics." *Global Dialogue: Newsletter for the International Sociological Association*, October 30, 2013. Accessed February 28, 2016. http://isa-global-dialogue.net/death-by-metrics/.

Howard, Douglas. "A Teaching Career in Fragments." *Chronicle of Higher Education*, February 24, 2014. Accessed February 28, 2016. http://chronicle.com/article/A-Teaching-Career-in-Fragments/144911.

Jaschik, Scott. "The Emails on Salaita." *Inside Higher Ed*, August 25, 2014. Accessed February 28, 2016. https://www.insidehighered.com/news/2014/08/25/u-illinois-officials-defend-decision-deny-job-scholar-documents-show-lobbying.

———. "Firing a Faculty Blogger." *Inside Higher Ed*, February 5, 2015. Accessed February 28, 2016. https://www.insidehighered.com/news/2015/02/05/marquette-moves-fire-controversial-faculty-blogger.

———. "The Professor Who Wasn't Fired." *Inside Higher Ed*, July 1, 2015. Accessed February 28, 2016. https://www.insidehighered.com/news/2015/07/01/twitter-explodes-false-reports-u-memphis-fired-professor-why.

———. "Saida Grundy, Moving Forward." *Inside Higher Ed*, August 24, 2015. Accessed February 28, 2016. https://www.insidehighered.com/news/2015/

08/24/saida-grundy-discusses-controversy-over-her-comments-twitter-her
-career-race-and.

Kahn, Richard, and Douglas Kellner. "New Media and Internet Activism: From the
'Battle of Seattle' to Blogging." *New Media & Society* 6, no. 1 (2004): 87–95.

Kalish, Ilene. "Great Books Aren't Written, They're Re-Written." *Contexts* 12, no. 3
(August 11, 2013): 88.

Kassens-Noor, Eva. "Twitter as a Teaching Practice to Enhance Active and Informal
Learning in Higher Education: The Case of Sustainable Tweets." *Active Learning in Higher Education* 13, no. 1 (2012): 9–21.

Kinner, Derek. "FSU Instructor Resigns after Folio Weekly Asks about Racist
Emails." *Folio Weekly*, December 8, 2014. Accessed February 28, 2016. http://
folioweekly.com/FSU-INSTRUCTOR-RESIGNS-AFTER-FOLIO-WEEKLY-ASKS
-ABOUT-RACIST-FACEBOOK-POSTS,11706.

Kleinman, Arthur. "Writing across Borders." Durham University, Department
of Anthropology, Writing across Boundaries, n.d. Accessed February 28,
2016. https://www.dur.ac.uk/writingacrossboundaries/writingonwriting/
arthurkleinman/.

Klinenberg, Eric. *Going Solo: The Extraordinary Rise and Surprising Appeal of Living
Alone.* New York: Penguin Press, 2012.

Kotlowitz, Alex. "Deep Cover: Review of on the Run." *New York Times*, Sunday Book
Review, June 29, 2014. Accessed February 28, 2016. http://www.nytimes.com/
2014/06/29/books/review/alice-goffmans-on-the-run.html.

Kuttner, Robert. "She Minds the Child, He Minds the Dog." *New York Times* Book
Review, June 25, 1989. Accessed February 28, 2016. http://www.nytimes.com/
1989/06/25/books/she-minds-the-child-he-minds-the-dog.html?pagewanted
=all.

Labi, Aisha. "Researchers Resist Pressure to Show Impact of Their Work." *Chronicle
of Higher Education*, February 9, 2014. Accessed February 28, 2016. http://
chronicle.com/article/Researchers-Resist-Pressure-to/144533/.

Lena, Jennifer. "Why Hipsters Hate on Lana Del Rey." *Pacific Standard*, December 9, 2012. Accessed February 28, 2016. http://www.psmag.com/books-and
-culture/lana-del-rey-hip-hop-grunge-rick-ross-authentic-music-50442.

Lepore, Jill. "The New Economy of Letters." *Chronicle of Higher Education*, September 3, 2013. Accessed February 28, 2016. http://chronicle.com/article/The
-New-Economy-of-Letters/141291/.

Lessig, Lawrence. *The Future of Ideas: The Fate of the Commons in a Connected World.*
New York: Vintage, 2002.

Lewin, Tamar. "Parents' Financial Support May Not Help College Grades." *New
York Times*, January 14, 2013. Accessed February 28, 2016. http://www.nytimes
.com/2013/01/15/education/parents-financial-support-linked-to-college
-grades.html?_r=0.

Lewis-Kraus, Gideon. "The Trials of Alice Goffman." *New York Times*, January 12,

2016. Accessed February 28, 2016. http://www.nytimes.com/2016/01/17/ magazine/the-trials-of-alice-goffman.html.

Löfgren, Orvar. "Routinising Research: Academic Skills in Analogue and Digital Worlds." *International Journal of Social Research Methodology* 17, no. 1 (2014): 73–86.

Lubet, Steven. "Ethics on the Run: Review of *On the Run: Fugitive Life in an American City* by Alice Goffman." *New Rambler Review*, 2015. Accessed February 28, 2016. http://newramblerreview.com/book-reviews/law/ethics-on-the-run.

Lupton, Deborah. *Digital Sociology.* New York: Routledge, 2014.

Mackey, Robert. "Professor's Angry Tweets on Gaza Cost Him His Job." *New York Times*, September 12, 2014. Accessed February 28, 2016. http://www.nytimes .com/2014/09/13/world/middleeast/professors-angry-tweets-on-gaza-cost -him-a-job.html.

MacPhail, Theresa. "The Art and Science of Finding Your Voice." *Chronicle of Higher Education*, August 8, 2014. Accessed February 28, 2016. https:// chroniclevitae.com/news/651-the-art-and-science-of-finding-your-voice.

Mason, Alane Salierno. "Nine Tips for Academics Writing for a General Audience." *W. W. Norton & Co.*, n.d. Accessed February 28, 2016. http://wwnorton.tumblr .com/post/32954793512/nine-tips-for-academics-writing-for-a-general.

Matthew, Patricia. "@triciamatthew 4 associate professor." *Written/Unwritten Blog*, July 6, 2014. Accessed February 28, 2016. https://writtenunwritten .wordpress.com/2014/07/06/triciamatthew-4-associate-professor/.

McGuire, Mark. "The Difficulty in Rating Transformational Experiences." *HASTAC Blog*, February 8, 2014. Accessed February 28, 2016. https://www.hastac .org/blogs/markmcguire/2014/02/08/difficulty-rating-transformational -experiences.

McNair, Beth. "Social Scientists Seek New Ways to Influence Public Policy." *Chronicle of Higher Education*, April 30, 2013. Accessed February 28, 2016. http://chronicle.com/article/Social-Scientists-Seek-New/141305.

Meyer, Dan. "Stanford History Education Professor Sam Wineburg Learns to Tweet." *Dy/Dan Blog*, February 18, 2013. Accessed February 28, 2016. http://blog.mrmeyer.com/2013/stanford-history-education-professor-sam -wineburg-learns-to-tweet/.

Milkman, Ruth. "A More Perfect Union." *New York Times*, June 30, 2005. Accessed February 28, 2016. http://www.nytimes.com/2005/06/30/opinion/a-more -perfect-union.html.

Mills, C. Wright. "On Intellectual Craftsmanship." Appendix to *The Sociological Imagination*. New York: Oxford University Press, 1959.

———. *The Sociological Imagination.* New York: Oxford University Press, 1959.

Mills, Katherine, and Pamela Mills, eds. *C. Wright Mills: Letters and Autobiographical Writings.* Berkeley: University of California Press, 2001.

Moore, Heidi N. "Why Is Thomas Piketty's 700-page Book a Bestseller?" *The Guard-*

ian, September 21, 2014. Accessed February 28, 2016. http://www.theguardian .com/money/2014/sep/21/-sp-thomas-piketty-bestseller-why.

Netherland, Julie. "Tips for Academics Who Want to Work with Policy Makers." *JustPublics@365*, October 24, 2013. Accessed February 28, 2016. http:// justpublics365.commons.gc.cuny.edu/2013/10/24/tips-academics-want-to -engage-policymakers/.

Okerson, Ann, and Clifford Lynch. "Pondering the Digital Dilemma: A Personal Reflection." *Against the Grain* 12, no. 3 (2013): 20.

Oladepo, Tomi. "The Digital Academic, a Changing Culture—Interview with Dr. Charlotte Mathieson." *Digital Media Culture*, October 21, 2014. Accessed February 28, 2016. http://digimediaculture.com/2014/10/21/the-digital -academic-a-changing-culture-interview/.

Open Access Institutional Repositories: A Briefing Paper, 2009. Liege, Belgium: Enabling Open Scholarship (EOS). Accessed February 28, 2016. http://www .openscholarship.org/upload/docs/application/pdf/2009–09/open_access_ institutional_repositories.pdf.

Pastor, Manuel, J. Ito, and Rachel Rosner. "Transactions—Transformations—Translations: Metrics That Matter for Building, Scaling, and Funding Social Movements." Report. Los Angeles: USC Program for Environmental and Regional Equity, 2011. Accessed February 28, 2016. http://bolderadvocacy.org/reco -resource/transactions-transformations-translations-metrics-that-matter-for -building-scaling-and-funding-social-movements.

Perry, Imani. "The New Black Public Intellectual." *Chronicle of Higher Education*, June 6, 2010. Accessed February 28, 2016. https://chronicle.com/article/The -New-Black-Public/65744/.

Piwowar, Heather. "Altmetrics: Value All Research Products." *Nature* 493 (January 10, 2013): 159. Accessed February 28, 2106. http://www.nature.com/ nature/journal/v493/n7431/full/493159a.html.

Priem, Jason, Kaitlin Costello, and Tyler Dzuba. "Prevalence and Use of Twitter among Scholars." In *Metrics: Symposium on Informetric and Scientometric Research* (2011). Figshare. Accessed February 28, 2016. http://dx.doi.org/10 .6084/m9.figshare.104629.

Priem, Jason, Dario Taraborelli, Paul Groth, and Cameron Neylon. "Altmetrics: Manifesto." *Altmetrics Blog* October 26, 2010. Accessed February 28, 2016. http://altmetrics.org/manifesto.

Putnam, Robert. *Bowling Alone: The Collapse and Revival of American Community.* New York: Simon and Schuster, 2000.

Rheingold, Howard. *Net Smart: How to Thrive Online.* Cambridge, MA: MIT Press, 2012.

———. "Twitter Literacy (I Refuse to Make Up a Twittery Name for It)." *SFGate*, May 11, 2009. Accessed August 22, 2015. http://blog.sfgate.com/rheingold/ 2009/05/11/twitter-literacy-i-refuse-to-make-up-a-twittery-name-for-it/.

Richardson, Morgane. "Interview with PJ Rey and Nathan Jurgenson." *JustPublics* @365, March 1, 2013. Accessed February 28, 2016. http://justpublics365 .commons.gc.cuny.edu/2013/03/01/an-interview-with-pj-nathan-founders -of-ttw13/.

Riesman, David. *The Lonely Crowd: A Study of the Changing American Character.* New Haven, CT: Yale University Press, 1950.

Ritzer, George. *Introduction to Sociology.* 2nd ed. Thousand Oaks, CA: Sage, 2014.

———. "Who's a Public Intellectual?" *British Journal of Sociology* 57, no. 2 (2006): 209–13.

Ronson, Jon. "How One Stupid Tweet Blew Up Justine Sacco's Life." *New York Times*, February 12, 2015. Accessed February 28, 2016. http://www.nytimes .com/2015/02/15/magazine/how-one-stupid-tweet-ruined-justine-saccos-life .html.

Saunders, George. Interview, Long Form podcast, January 15, 2014. Accessed February 28, 2016. http://longform.org/posts/longform-podcast-75-george -saunders.

Scanlon, Eileen. "Scholarship in the Digital Age: Open Educational Resources, Publication and Public Engagement." *British Journal of Educational Technology* 45, no. 1 (2014): 12–23.

Schmidt, Pete. "Twitter Casualty." *Chronicle of Higher Education*, December 15, 2014. Accessed February 28, 2016. http://www.chroniclecareers.com/article/2014 -INFLUENCE-LIST-TWITTER/150853/#sthash.ke2YsJ6P.dpuf.

Schuman, Rebecca. "Why Did This Marxist Philosopher Plagiarize a White Supremacist Magazine?" *Slate*, July 14, 2014. Accessed February 28, 2016. http:// www.slate.com/blogs/browbeat/2014/07/14/slavoj_zizek_plagiarized_white _supremacist_magazine_american_renaissance.html.

Schwartz, Pepper. *Everything You Know about Love and Sex Is Wrong.* New York: Perigree Books, 2001.

———. "Stage Fright or Death Wish: Sociology in the Mass Media" *Contemporary Sociology* 27, no. 5 (1998): 439–45.

Shapiro, Dani. "Memoir Is Not a Status Update." *New Yorker*, August 18, 2014. Accessed February 28, 2016. http://www.newyorker.com/culture/cultural -comment/memoir-status-update.

Sharpe, Christina. "Black Life—Annotated." *The New Inquiry*, August 8, 2014. Accessed February 28, 2016. http://thenewinquiry.com/essays/black-life -annotated/.

Shuai, Xin, Alberto Pepe, and Johan Bollen. "How the Scientific Community Reacts to Newly Submitted Preprints: Article Downloads, Twitter Mentions, and Citations." *PLoS ONE* 7, no. 11 (2012): e47523. Accessed February 28, 2016. doi:10.1371/journal.pone.0047523.

Smith-Cruz, Shawnta, Polly Thistlethwaite, and Jessie Daniels. "Open Scholarship for Open Education: Building the JustPublics@365 POOC." *Journal of*

Library Innovation 5, no. 2 (2014): 15. Accessed February 28, 2016. http://www
.libraryinnovation.org/article/view/370.

Starr, Terrell Jermaine. "The Unbelievable Harassment Black Women Face Daily on
Twitter." *Alternet*, September 16, 2014. Accessed on February 28, 2016. http://
www.alternet.org/unbelievable-harassment-black-women-face-daily-twitter.

Stein, Arlene. "Discipline and Publish: Public Sociology in an Age of Profes-
sionalization." In *Bureaucratic Culture and Escalating Problems: Advancing the
Sociological Imagination*, ed. David Knottnerus and Bernard Phillips, 156–71.
Boulder, CO: Paradigm Publishers, 2009.

———. "Sex, Truths, and Audiotape: Anonymity and the Effects of Exposure in
Public Ethnography." *Journal of Contemporary Ethnography* 39, no. 5 (October
2010): 554–68.

———. *The Stranger Next Door: The Story of a Small Community's Battle over Sex,
Faith, and Civil Rights*. Boston: Beacon, 2001.

Sternheimer, Karen. "The Mediated Sociologist." *Contexts* (Spring 2014): 56–58.

Stewart, Bonnie. "In Abundance: Networked Participatory Practices as Scholarship." *International Review of Research in Open and Distributed Learning* 16, no. 3
(2015). Accessed February 28, 2016. http://www.irrodl.org/index.php/irrodl/
article/view/2158/3343.

———. "Open to Influence: What Counts as Academic Influence in Scholarly Networked Twitter Participation." *Learning, Media and Technology* 40, no. 3 (2015):
1–23.

Stirland, Sarah Lai. "How a Trio of Feminists Persuaded Facebook to Unfriend
Rape 'Humor' Groups." *TechPresident*, May 30, 2013. Accessed February 28,
2016. http://techpresident.com/news/23945/how-trio-feminists-persuaded
-facebook-unfriend-rape-humor-groups.

Swartz, David L. "From Critical Sociology to Public Intellectual: Pierre Bourdieu
and Politics." *Theory and Society* 32, nos. 5–6 (2003): 791–823.

Tanner, Simon. "The Value and Impact of Digitized Resources for Learning, Teaching, Research and Enjoyment." In *Evaluating and Measuring the Value, Use and
Impact of Digital Collections*, ed. Lorna Hughes, 103–20. London: Facet Publishing, 2011.

Turner, Bryan S. "British Sociology and Public Intellectuals: Consumer Society and
Imperial Decline." *British Journal of Sociology* 57, no. 2 (2006): 169–88.

Uggen, Christopher, and Michelle Inderbitzin. "The Price and the Promise of
Citizenship: Extending the Vote to Nonincarcerated Felons." In *Contemporary
Issues in Criminal Justice Policy: Policy Proposals from the American Society of
Criminology Conference*, ed. Natasha A. Frost, Joshua D. Freilich, and Todd R.
Clear, 61–68. Belmont, CA: Cengage/Wadsworth, 2010.

VanBuren, Emily. "Should You Blog Your Dissertation Research?" *Inside Higher Ed*,
May 24, 2014. Accessed February 28, 2016. https://www.insidehighered.com/
blogs/gradhacker/open-thread-should-you-blog-your-dissertation-research.

vanden Heuvel, Katrina. "Jenny McCarthy's Vaccination Fear-Mongering and the Cult of False Equivalence." *Nation*, July 22, 2013. Accessed February 28, 2016. http://www.thenation.com/article/jenny-mccarthys-vaccination-fear -mongering-and-cult-false-equivalence/.

Veletsianos, George. "Higher Education Scholars' Participation and Practices on Twitter." *Journal of Computer Assisted Learning* 28, no. 4 (2012): 336–49.

Venkatesh, Sudhir. *Gang Leader for a Day*. New York: Penguin, 2008.

———. "Writing Outside the (Sociological) Box." *Contexts* 13, no. 2, (2014): 92.

Wade, Lisa, and Gwen Sharp. "Sociological Images Blogging as Public Sociology." *Social Science Computer Review* 31, no. 2 (2013): 221–28.

Walters, Suzanna Danuta. *The Tolerance Trap: How God, Genes, and Good Intentions Are Sabotaging Gay Equality*. New York: New York University Press, 2014.

Ward, Jane. *Not Gay: Sex between Straight White Men*. New York: New York University Press, 2015.

Weinstein, Adam. "FSU Lecturer Loses Job over Rant against 'Filthy Rodent Muslims.'" *Gawker*, December 10, 2014. Accessed February 28, 2016. http://gawker .com/fsu-lecturer-loses-job-over-rant-against-filthy-rodent-1669244536.

Weller, Katrin, Axel Bruns, Jean Burgess, Merja Mahrt, and Cornelius Puschmann, eds. *Twitter and Society*. New York: Peter Lang, 2013.

Williams, Owen. "The 18 Best Blogging and Publishing Platforms on the Internet Today." *The Next Web*, May 11, 2015. Accessed February 28, 2016. http:// thenextweb.com/businessapps/2015/05/11/the-18-best-blogging-and -publishing-platforms-on-the-internet-today/.

Wilsdon, James, Liz Allen, Eleonora Belfiore, Philip Campbell, Stephen Curry, Steven Hill, Richard Jones, et al. "The Metric Tide: Report of the Independent Review of the Role of Metrics in Research Assessment and Management." *Digital Education Resource Archive*, July 16, 2015. Accessed August 28, 2105. http://dera.ioe.ac.uk/23424/.

Wilson, John K. "How Money Mattered in the Salaita Case." *Academe Blog*, January 6, 2015. Accessed February 28, 2016. http://academeblog.org/2015/01/06/ how-money-mattered-in-the-salaita-case/.

Wingfield, Nick. "Feminist Critics of Video Games Facing Threats in 'Gamergate' Campaign." *New York Times*, October 15, 2014. Accessed February 28, 2016. http://www.nytimes.com/2014/10/16/technology/gamergate-women-video -game-threats-anita-sarkeesian.html.

Young, Jeffrey R. "Teaching with Twitter: Not for the Faint of Heart." *Education Digest: Essential Readings Condensed for Quick Review* 75, no. 7 (2010): 9–12.

Zuckerman, Phil. *Living the Secular Life: New Answers to Old Questions*. New York: Penguin, 2014.

Index